RIGHTNOW

RIGHTNOW

A 12-STEP PROGRAM FOR DEFEATING THE OBAMA AGENDA

MICHAEL STEELE

Since 1947
REGNERY
PUBLISHING, INC.
An Eagle Publishing Company • Washington, DC

Library of Congress Cataloging-in-Publication Data
Steele, Michael S.
  Right now : a 12-step program for defeating the Obama agenda / Michael Steele.
    p. cm.
  ISBN 978-1-59698-108-9
  1. Republican Party (U.S. : 1854-) 2. Conservatism—United States.
3. United States—Politics and government—2009- 4. United States—Economic policy—2009 5. United States—Social policy—1993- 6. United States—Military policy. I. Title.
  JK2356.S74 2009
  324.2734—dc22

                                                              2009041039

Published in the United States by

Regnery Publishing, Inc.
One Massachusetts Avenue, NW
Washington, DC 20001
www.regnery.com

Manufactured in the United States of America

10 9 8 7 6 5 4 3 2 1

Books are available in quantity for promotional or premium use. Write to Director of Special Sales, Regnery Publishing, Inc., One Massachusetts Avenue NW, Washington, DC 20001, for information on discounts and terms or call (202) 216-0600.

Distributed to the trade by:
Perseus Distribution
387 Park Avenue South
New York, NY 10016

TO EVERYONE who's ever licked a stamp
or stuffed an envelope on behalf of the
Republican Party—this book
is dedicated to you.

CONTENTS

ACKNOWLEDGMENTS

WITH ALL the challenges and obstacles we have faced and will face in the future, I am proudest of the one thing the Republican Party has that matters most: you. You and Republican activists like you all across this country know a better path to take.

That path, a part of our mission since 1854, is simply to empower the people of this great nation.

In writing this book, I have been empowered by so many individuals who in unique and sometimes extraordinary ways embody the very spirit of America as that "shining city on a hill." They have been a shining light for me.

I learned a long time ago that nothing gets done without a strong woman leading the way. My wife Andrea told me that. And she was right. Her quiet encouragement and support are manifest in the writing of this "great adventure." Everyone needs someone to help them "keep it real." Andrea has done that and more for me. I remember the night I lost the race for the U.S. Senate in 2006. There we sat on the edge of the hotel bed watching the returns and my race slip into history. After several moments I wondered out loud, "What should I do now?" Andrea responded, "I guess you better get a job."

Nothing like keeping it real. Thank you, Andrea.

The things you learn from your children sometimes surprise you as well. Certainly my own boys, Michael and Drew, have taught me about tapping into one's creative nature and exhibiting the discipline to get the job done. Michael (the animator) and Drew (the writer) have each inspired me to get this done. Thank you, fellas; and Drew, your book is next!

I also want to thank my friend and colleague, Michael E. Long. Mike is of the grassroots. His guidance, suggestions, and passion for America and our party helped me capture in words the way forward.

An effort like this cannot get done (along with everything else one has to do) without a "Belinda"! So, to my personal assistant and central organizer, Belinda Cook, thank you!

And to "The Team"—Randy Evans, Stefan Passantino, and Kathy Lubbers—who demonstrated faith in me and the story I wanted to share, thank you for helping me launch this first effort.

And a very special thank you to the countless CRs, YRs, TARs, members of the National Federation of Republican Women, and the wonderful members of our party's grassroots whom I've met, laughed with, and cried with over the years. You have been the true light to inspire the words in this book.

Because of you, we now have an unprecedented opportunity to give America a new direction, a new vision, a truer appreciation of what it means for America once again to be that shining city on a hill.

FOREWORD

by Newt Gingrich

RECENTLY, I spoke at an event emceed by the accomplished actor and all-around great American John Voigt. During the evening, we were treated to a few scenes from one of John's movies in which, ironically, he portrays a Democrat: President Franklin Delano Roosevelt.

In one of these scenes, Voigt, as Roosevelt, is sitting in a meeting with many of his generals and advisors, and they are explaining to him why an operation the scale of the landing at Normandy could not be accomplished.

In reaction, Roosevelt silences the room by hoisting himself up from his wheelchair so that he is standing at the end of the table. (Remember, Roosevelt has been paralyzed from the waist down since 1921.) Dramatically, in a booming voice, Roosevelt intones, "Don't tell me it can't be done!"

In the wake of the election losses of 2006 and 2008, it occurred to me that the phrase "Don't tell me it can't be done" is the perfect battle cry for Republicans. After all, we have been here before.

In 1964, Republican Barry Goldwater lost a devastating election to Democrat Lyndon Johnson by over 20 percentage points. Republicans also lost 36 seats in the House and 3 seats in the

Senate. Everyone thought the Republican Party was finished. But in 1966, Republicans rebounded with a 47-seat gain in the House and a 3-seat gain in the Senate. Then, two years later, Republican Richard Nixon won the presidency.

In 1974, fresh on the heels of the Watergate scandal, Democrats gained 49 seats in the House, giving them a veto-proof majority, as well as 3 seats in the Senate. Two years later, Democrat Jimmy Carter won a narrow victory over Republican Gerald Ford, giving Democrats the House, Senate, and presidency. Once again, all the pundits and "experts" proclaimed that the Republican Party was finished.

Of course, we know how foolish that prediction would prove to be. In 1980, Republican Ronald Reagan won a landslide election against President Carter. In addition, Republicans gained 35 seats in the House and a remarkable 12 seats in the Senate, shifting control of the Senate to Republicans for the first time in 26 years.

In 1992, incumbent Republican President George H. W. Bush lost to Democrat Bill Clinton, and Democrats again controlled the House, Senate, and presidency. Not surprisingly, the conventional wisdom was that the Republican Party was over.

We proved them wrong in 1994 with the Contract with America campaign, resulting in a 54-seat pickup in the House (the largest in history) and an 8-seat pickup in the Senate, giving Republicans the majority in both chambers. In 1996, even though President Clinton was reelected, Republicans maintained control of both chambers and remained the dominant party in Washington until the 2006 elections.

So indeed, for those who again doubt the Republican Party can return to a majority, "Don't tell me it can't be done." It has been done before, and we can do it again. In fact, the recent election of Republican governors in New Jersey, supposedly an irreversibly blue state, and in Virginia show that patience is already wearing thin with the Democrats' overreaching Big Government agenda.

There is a clear road back to a majority, and this book illuminates it. The American people will take care of the Republican Party if the Republican Party takes care of the American people. This means we must offer better solutions consistent with the quintessentially American, free-market, pro-family, pro-freedom values that we share with the vast majority of the American people. This country is an overwhelmingly center-right nation. As Michael Steele urges, Republicans just need the courage and clarity to communicate these shared values effectively.

For those who doubt that Republicans can quickly return to being a governing majority, consider the opportunity in California, a reliably "blue" state where registered Democrats outnumber Republicans by almost 2 million voters.

Indeed, in the 2008 election, then Senator Obama received 61 percent of the vote in California. But just six months later in May, an even larger majority of Californians, 64 percent, defeated a series of ballot initiatives that would have raised taxes and increased spending. Even in San Francisco, a district held by Speaker Nancy Pelosi, 51 percent voted against these initiatives.

Think about what these results mean. They mean that even in the most liberal district in the United States, there is a majority to be gained around the principles of fiscal responsibility, limited government, and lower taxes. But this opportunity also illustrates the fundamental challenge for Republicans.

If we are to successfully arouse this coalition around a series of positive reforms, it means Republicans will need to be inclusive, not exclusive. Remember, President Ronald Reagan always began his speeches by addressing "My fellow Republicans, and those independents and Democrats who are looking for a better future." There were not enough Republicans to win in 1980, so Reagan won by attracting independents and Democrats.

That means Republicans must be willing to go into "blue" areas like San Francisco, Detroit, and Chicago and vigorously declare our values. It means making a real and sustained effort at communicating with African-Americans and Latinos. It also means being willing to tolerate differences of opinion within the party. After all, a Republican Party that carries San Francisco is inevitably going to have lots of internal debates. That is the nature of majorities.

To be clear, inclusion does not mean lack of principles. In 1975, after the post-Watergate Democratic landslide, Ronald Reagan encouraged conservatives to raise a "banner of no pale pastels, but bold colors." We once again need bold colors to reinvigorate our movement. Our solutions must be clear enough and bold enough to make it evident how different we are than the Left and to cut through the mainstream media's leftwing bias and trivial obsessions.

Some will argue that Republicans don't have to offer better solutions, that it is okay to be the "Party of No" against the agenda of President Obama, Speaker Pelosi, and Senator Reid.

This strategy may sometimes work as a way to get elected. But once elected, what mandate would we have for reform? In 1994, Republicans ran on the Contract with America, ten positive reforms that the country overwhelmingly supported. Not only did it work as an election strategy, it worked as a governing strategy. Nine out of ten items in the Contract passed the House of Representatives. We cut taxes, reformed welfare, saved Medicare from bankruptcy, and increased defense spending while balancing the budget and paying off more than $400 billion in debt. Amazingly, we did this with a liberal Democrat as president. If we had not run on a clear and bold agenda for reform, this success would not have been possible.

Right Now convincingly argues that it's once again time for bold colors.

America's economy is in desperate shape. We are recovering too slowly from the housing bubble's collapse and the financial crisis. Jobs continue to be shed. The nearly $800 billion stimulus package, passed by Congress in haste without reading it, has proven to be merely a collection of payoffs for politicians, a way for state governments to avoid making hard spending decisions. It has failed. Worse, any future recovery is in peril due to the massive new deficits caused by the Obama administration's reckless spending.

Abroad, America's enemies are on the march. The Taliban is resurgent in Afghanistan. Iran and North Korea are moving ahead with their nuclear weapons and missile programs. Russia is acting increasingly hostile. Strongmen dictators in South America are solidifying control. The drug war in Mexico is spilling across the border, endangering American lives. Sadly, the Obama administration's response to these threats has been weakness. They have wavered on our commitment to victory in Afghanistan and capitulated to Russia by cancelling missile defense in Eastern Europe.

Additionally, the Obama administration has joined the dictators Hugo Chavez and Fidel Castro in actively supporting the socialist Manuel Zelaya, the former Honduran President who was lawfully removed from office by the Honduran government for violating their constitution.

Beyond the immediate mistakes of the current leftwing administration and Congress, there are long-term challenges. If Americans are to remain the most safe, most prosperous, and most free people on the planet in the twenty-first century, we will need fundamental reform of litigation, regulation, taxation, education, energy, health, and infrastructure to compete with China and India. This level of change will require a movement that rallies our center-right nation to impose its will on the entrenched interest groups that survive off of the status quo. It will need to stretch beyond the Republican Party to once again include "those independents and Democrats who want a better future."

We stand for a strong national and homeland security system. We stand for a solid base in classic American principles. We can offer far better solutions than the Left. It is definitely time for "no pale pastels, but bold colors" once again.

Michael Steele's *Right Now* does a perfect job of raising this rallying cry. This book doesn't just expose the Left's radical vision for America's future; it successfully contrasts it with an attractive alternative vision that respects the dignity of the individual over the convenience of the state. It should be read by all our "fellow Republicans" who want to participate in what Chairman Steele boldly calls the coming Republican Renaissance.

PART
ONE

WHAT WENT WRONG

Republicans gave in to big government, and we paid the price. The road forward is clear: we need to reclaim conservative values.

STEPS

1 and 2

Admit We Have a Problem,
Then Admit Our Mistakes

CONSERVATIVES across the country have raised their voices loud and clear in the past six months, with tea parties and townhall meetings and two resounding victories in New Jersey and Virginia. They've looked at what's going on in Washington, D.C., and they've said: enough is *enough*.

Enough of a federal government whose liberal leaders are gleefully tearing down the economic foundations of capitalism.

Enough of the arrogant liberal lie that we can tax and spend and borrow our way back to prosperity.

Enough of mortgaging our children's future on "stimulus" packages that are mostly pork, political paybacks, and the tax-payer-funded delivery of a long-awaited wish list from the Democratic Party.

Enough of the liberal thought police who label anyone who disagrees with them a criminal or a bigot.

Enough of the leftist fantasy that we can negotiate with terrorists who want us dead.

But you know what else? Enough of Republican politicians who let them get away with it!

Enough of the one-sided compromises.

Enough of running from our principles.

Enough of *forgetting* our principles.

Enough of complaining about big government when we're out of power, but embracing big government when we're in power.

What in the world has happened to Republicans' conservative principles?

_____

Now more than ever, the Left in America is openly attacking the foundations of the American experiment. They believe the government is not only smarter than the individual, but is also entitled to make all manner of decisions on behalf of the individual. They believe real freedom isn't doing what you want to do, it's doing what government lets you do.

They brook virtually no disagreement on issue or philosophy, and they enforce this hegemony through the most influential positions of power in America: the presidency, majorities in the House and Senate, activist judges, the print and broadcast media, and the academic community.

Every day they do their dead-level best to convince Americans that freedom isn't *really* about being free. They demand influence in every purchase and sale, in what you do for a living and how you do it, in how you interact with your community, in what you spend and how much you give away. They chip away at our freedom, surrendering more and more of your individual rights in service to the "best interests" of some larger group.

Of course, the liberals decide what those "best interests" are—never mind what we want for ourselves and our families.

To the American Left, freedom is now defined as falling in line with elites who are quick to vilify any dissent—and that is not exactly an invitation to reasoned debate. To disagree with the Left today is to invite a withering personal attack on one's character.

They're free to do that, of course. Unlike a growing number of liberals, conservatives defend the right of everyone to speak their mind. The problem with growing liberal authority is that lately it includes a concerted attempt to limit their opponents' right to express a dissenting opinion. Look at the support from Democratic senators like John Kerry, Dick Durbin, and others for reinstating the Fairness Doctrine in order to muzzle conservative talk radio. Check out the Obama administration's demonization of Fox News. Or consider the Justice Department's decision to drop the case against members of the New Black Panther Party who stood guard on Election Day at a Philadelphia voting precinct—with one Panther carrying a truncheon—in order to intimidate voters from choosing the "wrong" candidate.

This administration's view of its political opponents was perhaps best captured in the Department of Homeland Security's

2009 report recommending that military veterans, pro-life groups, and opponents of unrestricted immigration be watched as potential domestic terrorists. (As the *Washington Examiner* later revealed, the report used "reliable" sources such as a fringe website specializing in warnings about the approaching end of the world.)

The Left has gone off the rails. Where once both sides of the American political conversation defended vigorous debate, the Left now seeks "enforced consensus" and groupthink—they rarely consider opinions other than their own. Today, everyone knows the consequences of dissent against the Left: to disagree in even the smallest way is not only to invite the label "closed-minded," but also, allegedly, to be filled with hate and rage.

Just ask any of the tea party demonstrators or healthcare "reform" protestors. These are typical, tax-paying Americans who join together to appeal for responsible spending policies and limited government. In response, they have been maligned by Democratic leaders and much of the mainstream media as dangerous, hate-filled extremists. Sometimes denouncing them as a "mob," other times (in contradiction) condemning them as part of a phony Astroturf campaign, the liberal establishment, after years of engaging in the most vitriolic attacks on President Bush, has suddenly discovered the supreme value of civility—and the need to enforce it.

Yet liberalism doesn't deserve all the blame for our economic decline, the diminished priority of American security, and falling support for the right to speak one's mind.

The other half of the equation is this: Republicans stopped putting up a fight.

Not all of us gave up the fight and not all the time. But many, especially among our leaders, have in recent years allowed our principles to be buried under layers of compromise or outright abandonment in the name of power and acceptance and going along to get along.

It's understandable how we got here: check the newspapers, the TV, and the Internet. The last decade has seen a withering and unyielding assault on all things conservative—a fire hose blast of invective, name-calling, and abuse from every angle. It has been exhausting to be a conservative!

But the fact that the fight is hard doesn't excuse us from combat.

After the historic transformation of our nation under President Ronald Reagan, how did we end up so far from our principles—and how did it happen so fast?

Republicans once insisted that our nation's opportunities rest not in government but in the hands of individuals. Over the past decade or so, however, we Republicans lost our way. The disparity between our rhetoric and our action grew until our credibility snapped. It wasn't the fault of our ideals. It was the failure of our leaders to live up to them.

Over time, many of our party's leaders abandoned conservative principles in a misguided effort to maintain and expand their political influence. We became in many ways just another party of big government. In short, we behaved like Democrats.

True, the country has changed, and our party must adapt. It is wrong, however, to believe we must change our principles or adopt "conservatism-lite." After all, the voters did not suddenly become liberal. They simply lost confidence that the Republican Party holds the answers to their problems.

We must articulate a positive vision for America's future that speaks to Americans' hopes, concerns, and needs. It's time to tell voters what we believe, how we'll lead, and where we'll go. We need to explain how we Republicans will help working families to keep more of what they earn; expand the options for their children's education; protect and improve their healthcare; encourage private businesses to create more jobs; restore fiscal responsibility to government; and make all of us safer from domestic and foreign threats.

Our challenge lies not only in defeating Democrats, but also in uniting around a message that solidifies our ranks and attracts new adherents to our cause. We have to listen to what Americans are telling us about their aspirations, and then translate that message into proposals for meaningful action squarely grounded on the values for which we Republicans have always stood.

We are united by our faith in the power and ingenuity of the individual to build a nation through hard work, personal responsibility, and self-discipline. That is the sacred ground upon which our Republican Party was built. For the sake of all Americans, it is the ground we must reclaim.

We Republicans can get some perspective on our recent problems by looking back at one of our finest hours: from 1981 to 1989, conservatism made real progress in rolling back the relentless advance of liberalism. Ronald Reagan's landslide victory in

1980, the president's warm and easy-going style, and his common-sense delivery of conservative wisdom changed everything. Ronald Reagan made it cool to be a Republican—at least for a time.

The Reagan victory was the culmination of a conservative rise that began in the ashes of a crushing defeat decades before. Throughout the 1980s, President Reagan and Republicans in Congress, along with some conservative Democrats, implemented a conservative agenda that had been groomed for twenty years: lowering taxes; cutting back the influence of government in personal life and private enterprise; promoting free markets over crippling regulation; standing up for individual rights and human rights over authoritarian repression; and the greatest victory of all, challenging the Soviet Union and winning the Cold War.

President Reagan made America and the world safer, more prosperous, and freer. This isn't a matter of opinion but a matter of fact by any measure: he set the stage for the transformation of formerly Communist police states into capitalist democracies; grew our gross domestic product; raised employment; reduced inflation; and much more. Few deny this anymore, and those who do might as well deny the sunrise.

But what many often forget is that President Reagan did what he did for all Americans and not for the elevation of the Republican Party. Moreover, he did it with the support of many Democrats in Congress—the so-called "Boll Weevils"—who recognized that their beliefs were much closer to Reagan's traditional Americanism than to those of their own increasingly left-leaning party. Those who knew the president would tell you this kind of inclusiveness and outreach was entirely in his character. He even had a sign on his desk that read:

> THERE IS NO LIMIT TO WHAT YOU
> CAN ACCOMPLISH IF YOU DON'T CARE
> WHO GETS THE CREDIT.

He employed Republican principles, but he didn't preach to the public about the wonders of being a Republican. Instead, he spoke consistently about common sense, about how to fix the problems that typical Americans faced every day, and about his concern for families and individuals. He didn't attempt to "sell" people into some "club" called Republicanism. He offered solutions to real-world problems, and those solutions were founded in rock-solid principle.

So how did the Republican Party benefit from Reagan? That's easy. People knew their president was a Republican, and they embraced the Republican label, not because of what Reagan-era Republicans said, but because of what they did. Simple as that.

After Reagan's presidency, however, our fortunes declined. Many post-Reagan Republican leaders were not nearly as confident in or committed to conservative principles, and not nearly as capable as Reagan was of living without the validation of the media and the chattering classes. Less than two years after Reagan left office, a Republican president raised taxes. And our party—and nation—paid a high price: in 1992, the American people voted to replace President George H. W. Bush with Bill Clinton, beginning only the second Democratic administration in twenty-four years. Despite the ensuing success of Congress-men Newt Gingrich's and Dick Armey's Contract with Amer-ica—with which they captured fifty-four seats in the House of Representatives and a Republican majority for the first time in more than half a century—many Republicans perversely wanted to emulate Clinton's electoral success by triangulating and run-ning as "moderates." They thought the key to winning elections was to run on watered-down conservatism.

So long was Reagan's shadow that seven years after the end of Reagan's term, President Clinton was forced to declare before Congress that "the era of big government is over." Yet four years later, many conservative leaders replied with, "Not yet." We would go along with big government, but we would just turn its priorities a little more toward free markets—and we would apologize for doing even that. Throughout the 2000s, we acquiesced to "bridges to nowhere," a return to deficits and expanding debt, growing government influence in healthcare, and the list goes on.

It didn't have to be this way. If you took what the Republican Congress did during President Clinton's tenure and applied that to the 2000s—holding the line on taxes, real reform of the safety net, balancing the budget—then recent Republican history would have been quite different.

Before we catalogue what exactly went wrong in the last decade, we have to remember that President George W. Bush and Republicans at all levels of government had some great achievements. Most important, they helped keep our nation safe from further attack after the devastation of September 11. The president made some profoundly difficult decisions to ensure the safety of our country, and he deserves thanks from all Americans, not just from Republicans.

But as the memory of September 11 receded, President Bush was subjected to unprecedented abuse from an increasingly angry American Left. Many liberals engaged in perpetual and vicious personal attacks solely in an attempt to tear down a Republican president. It became depressingly common to read of liberals fantasizing about President Bush's assassination—in fact, an entire movie was filmed about it.

It took a man of real character to stand up to years of withering assault and not back down. He kept America's defense as his top priority despite all the vitriol. He never considered trading our security for a moment of approval from a powerful leftwing movement blind with rage and lusting for power. For that, America owes George W. Bush a debt we cannot repay.

On the domestic front, Republicans ushered in a decade of across-the-board tax cuts that created jobs, spurred investment, and increased the take-home pay of working families. The president cut the marginal tax rate in every bracket—he didn't simply cut taxes "for the wealthy," as liberals falsely charge—and he expanded the lowest tax bracket so more people could pay less to the government. He lowered the tax burden on families by eliminating the marriage penalty and increasing the child tax credit.

What's more, tax cuts in 2003 raised the economy out of its post-September 11 decline. After the tax cuts, investment rose, the S&P increased by nearly a third, GDP shot up from an anemic 1.7 percent to 4.1 percent, and after a quarter-million lost jobs in the previous six quarters, the economy added 5 million jobs in less than two years.

Additionally, Republicans proposed practical, conservative solutions to the problems Americans faced. Chief among these initiatives was an attempt—killed by Democrats—to make Social Security solvent and head off its impending bankruptcy. Republicans also helped put impartial judges on our courts, including the Supreme Court. Refusing the temptation to legislate from the bench, these justices uphold their constitutional mandate to interpret law as legislators wrote it. And they promote equal treatment under the law—unlike President Obama, who insists Supreme Court justices should consider not only the law, but how they personally *feel* about the plaintiffs and defendants before them. Finally, the influence of principled Republicans in the House and Senate, especially since our party became the minority, has helped trim some of the worst excesses from liberal legislation.

But Republicans made some awful mistakes in recent years, too—departures from principle, often in the wrong-headed belief that occasional compromise of our core ideas could give us a strategic advantage or, even worse, could help Republicans stay in office. From today's perspective, it's clear those choices were wrong.

Don't believe the pundits' common refrain that the Republican Party has moved too far to the right. In reality, the problem is that we've been moving to the left. Here's why we've fallen out of touch with typical Americans: we've acquiesced to big government, big spending, and increased federal control that diminishes the authority of families and the rights of individuals. On entitlements, education, healthcare, immigration—even occasionally on free speech, free association, and free markets—we have compromised, caved, and collapsed.

It's time to do something that folks in politics rarely do: admit we were wrong. I'm not going to give you any of that song-and-dance that "mistakes were made" or "if someone misunderstood what we intended. . . ." Those are the weasel-word excuses that politicians say when they refuse to own up to their mistakes.

As chairman of the Republican National Committee, let me say it as clearly and succinctly as I can: we screwed up.

It wasn't that the entire party staged a mass exodus from principle; it was a relatively small number of Republicans and for a relatively brief period of time. But it happened enough times on enough key issues to damage our party's reputation and credibility. You can't build up big government and advance conservatism at the same time—it's one or the other. Yet on too many occasions, a significant number of Republicans tried in vain to square that circle. They tortured common sense to claim that this or that expansion of federal authority was entirely consistent with conservative principles.

Note that this is not a call for "ideological purity." No one should try to dispatch this or that group from our party. We need to draw people to us, not find reasons to send them away. But to attract people to our party, we have to offer something they can identify with—something they can believe in. Why would anyone be attracted to a party that doesn't stick to its principles?

In fact, there is an even better reason to stick to what we believe—our ideas work. Think of it this way: conservative principles produce policies that empower people. In contrast, liberal principles teach people that they're victims who can only be rescued by the latest federal program. Liberalism teaches people to give up. That ought to be easy to beat—but we caved anyway.

Here are some of the issues where we most glaringly compromised our principles:

WE WRONGLY BUILT UP BIG GOVERNMENT WITH BIG SPENDING.

From 2001 to 2004, while the federal government was under mostly Republican control, discretionary spending (that is, optional spending—what's not mandated by law) rose by almost 50 percent. In other words, for every dollar we were spending in 2001, we were spending $1.50 by 2004.

Through 2006, the adjusted annual increase in discretionary spending was 5.3 percent—nearly three times the 1.9 percent rate under President Reagan. Granted, America had to pay for wars in Afghanistan and Iraq during part of this time. But compare that figure to the 4.6 percent rate under President Lyndon Johnson, who also had to fund a war—we were outspending the Democrat who launched the liberals' centerpiece attempt at social engineering, the so-called "Great Society" programs.

For a party claiming that the federal government is often an impediment to the hopes and dreams of Americans, Republicans sure spent a lot of money trying to prove the opposite. According to the watchdog group Citizens Against Government Waste (CAGW)—a small-government advocate that had once cheered many Republican ideas—Congress passed nearly

77,000 earmarks between 2002 and 2009, comprising almost $172 billion in spending.

Of course, in the multi-trillion-dollar stimulating world of President Obama, a few billion here and there is a drop in the bucket. And over the last decade, Democrats were grabbing all the pork they could, too—it wasn't just Republicans bringing home the bacon. But Republicans controlled Congress for much of this period. They could have said no, and they did not—not with a unified, principled voice. Not as a party.

With President Bush failing to veto a single spending bill for the first five years of his presidency, Republicans became enablers for big government: there was the $286 billion "highway bill" of 2005, notable for its nearly 6,400 pet projects that channeled hundreds of millions of dollars to frivolous programs. There was the 2002 farm bill that drew government deeper into private farming. And there was the disappointing attempt to "make up" for the handling of Hurricane Katrina by trying to outspend the Democrats in its aftermath. Finally, we helped expand government-funded healthcare in a way the liberals by themselves couldn't have achieved back then. Any Republicans who thought liberals would be satisfied with that expansion must be sorely disappointed right now.

WE WRONGLY APPROVED THE TARP BAILOUTS.

When the financial crisis hit hard in 2008, the politicians panicked, clear and simple. The bill finally came due for companies that for years had been making bad decisions that exposed them to excessive risks, a process propelled by onerous government regulations. As the effects of the crisis rippled through the economy, a lot of our party leaders went along with the conventional wisdom that only massive government intervention would stave off a devastating economic collapse.

We really should have known better, but the dire rhetoric coming from the proponents of government intervention stoked deep fear. President Bush famously declared he'd "abandoned free market principles to save the free market system." The result was the creation of the Troubled Asset Relief Program (TARP)— a $700 billion behemoth of a government program to prop up troubled financial institutions.

It will be a long time before liberals admit that the global financial crisis was driven by political correctness and Democratic policy dating back to the Carter administration, when liberals in Congress passed the Community Reinvestment Act (CRA). That act forced banks to make risky home loans to under-qualified borrowers. Some people questioned the wisdom of encouraging home purchases by people who probably couldn't pay for them. But these cautious voices were denounced for being "against the poor" and "against African-Americans." Groups like ACORN, the community organizers extraordinaire, orchestrated boycotts and protests to force banks to reduce their credit standards. With the government pressuring banks in the same direction, the key elements of the subprime meltdown were put in place, especially when the government began more aggressively enforcing banks' CRA compliance under the Clinton administration.

Left with houses they could not afford, a lot of people defaulted on their mortgages or simply walked away from them, causing big losses to the banks. Quasi-government lenders Fannie Mae and Freddie Mac, which were perhaps the most irresponsible companies of them all, showed early signs of strain, but congressional Democrats, especially Congressman Barney Frank, insisted nothing was wrong; they even helped to kill Bush administration initiatives to clean up the mess before it became a global crisis. Frank and others believed their politically correct goal was too important to be tripped up by a little thing like economic reality.

Of course, it didn't take long for reality to set in. Banks began failing, then insurers of banks started failing, then companies dependent on banks began failing—and since most companies depend on banks to some extent, the fallout spread quickly. Other intrusive government regulations, such as requirements for mark-to-market accounting, created perverse incentives that weakened companies and added to the meltdown. The entire process was accelerated by poor decision-making by the financial institutions themselves, which imagined the explosion in housing prices would last forever and assumed even more risk than they were forced to assume by government regulations.

The Bush administration passed TARP to stem the crisis. The original idea was to stabilize financial institutions by buying up their toxic assets. But no sooner was the program approved than it began growing into a much more ambitious and more controlling enterprise. The government began choosing banks that would be "recapitalized" with taxpayer money. It subjected TARP recipients to debilitating oversight, insisted on a say in firms' key decisions, and took over ownership shares in some banks. Firms that didn't even need TARP cash were pressured to take it, and some companies met government resistance when they wanted to repay the money quickly—it seemed some officials were less interested in helping these businesses than in securing a way to own them for good. Finally, although designed to help financial institutions, TARP funds were tapped by the Bush administration to bail out Chrysler and General Motors to the tune of $23 billion. This opened the door to an even more radical government intervention in these companies by the Obama administration, as described in Step 3.

The Congressional Oversight Panel reported a disturbing lack of transparency and accountability in the TARP program. What do you expect? It's a giant government program. Moreover, in August 2009 the panel reported that hardly any TARP money was actually spent on buying toxic assets. "It is likely that an overwhelming portion of the troubled assets from last October remain on bank balance sheets today," the panel found, warning that these assets could lead to another financial crisis. Having failed to fulfill its original mandate, TARP, in effect, became a massive government slush fund used to support companies the government likes and force them to make decisions the government wants.

Now, I'm not saying there was nothing the government could do to help the economy. But it should have worked out a more careful, targeted, and transparent program designed to minimize job losses, maintain sources of capital for expansion, promote stability in global markets, keep the deficit from exploding, and help small businesses—the so-called "soft landing" that received a good deal of support from both Republicans and Democrats.

Lawmakers should have allowed risk-takers in the market to sustain the outcome of the bad risks they chose to take—the purchase of risky mortgages, bad debt, and complex financial instruments of dubious worth. This is true not just of big business and big banks, but also of individuals; if you buy a house you can't possibly afford, you don't deserve to have your neighbors pick up the tab for the difference between what you want and what you can actually pay for. But by deeming all kinds of companies "too big to fail," the government reduced the sobering power of moral hazard and risk throughout the whole economy.

Of course, government policy forced financial institutions to take on some of this excessive risk in the first place. But a healthy system does not force companies to engage in economically destructive activities, then use taxpayer money to save them from the consequences. A better policy minimizes government inter-ference, allows companies to make their own decisions, and lets firms stand or fall on their own accord.

The market recovery was going to entail pain no matter what. That pain—that price—hasn't been eliminated; the government just borrowed (and printed) money against our children's future so we wouldn't have to pay the price today. The federal govern-ment picked up the check for careless business executives, then divided it among current and future taxpayers. These executives and their businesses had friends in high places with access to tax-payer money and the will to use it.

TARP sent a dangerous message to corporate America: if you're "too big to fail," or if you've just got powerful friends, you don't have to worry about running your company well; if you drive it into the ground, the government will be here to bail you out, just like it was before.

WE WRONGLY SUPPORTED THE LARGEST NEW ENTITLEMENT IN HISTORY.

The Congressional Budget Office (CBO) estimates total Medicare expenditures for 2008 were $456 billion, which is about 15 percent of the nearly $3 trillion federal budget for that year. The CBO now forecasts that Medicare spending will nearly double in a decade. Republicans helped grow that spending thanks to the passage of one of the largest federal entitlement programs in history, the Medicare Part D prescription drug subsidy.

The entitlement didn't just accommodate those without coverage, it was for everybody—thus Medicare Part D tore down private coverage that already worked. When the measure passed in 2003 (it took effect on January 1, 2006), at least three-quarters of Medicare beneficiaries already had drug coverage. Millions of seniors lost their employer-provided drug coverage, and those who didn't lose it entirely found their existing coverage scaled back.

And that wasn't all. For many retired employees, the now-defunct coverage had been a benefit they had paid for throughout their careers. Instead of negotiating for salary increases or other benefits over the years, they accepted lesser compensation knowing they were, in effect, purchasing in advance a part of the healthcare coverage they would use during their retirement. The passage of Medicare Part D meant that whatever they "saved" through fewer benefits and a lower salary was sacrificed for nothing. Employers keep the money they saved to pay for this benefit because the government is going to send the bill to taxpayers instead.

Republicans didn't set out to grow an already massive entitlement. To the contrary, many conservatives set out to reform Medicare by introducing more market forces into healthcare and by promoting competition between Medicare and private insurance—competition that would lower healthcare costs, increase coverage choices, and raise the quality of care. Prescription drug coverage was the "sweetener"—what Republicans offered Democrats in exchange for introducing market reforms that might have reduced the long-term federal role in healthcare.

But by the time all the political horse-trading was through, the "sweetener" was all that was left in the bill—it was just another enjoy-it-now-pay-for-it-later benefit. Market-based reforms had been bartered away long before the floor vote. Having enticed the public with a tempting offer—now no longer tied to free-market principles—Republicans voted for a reform-free entitlement that the CBO estimates will cost nearly $11 trillion in today's dollars over seventy-five years of the program. And with the support of willing Republicans, an unprecedented expansion of federal control over healthcare—paid for by tax dollars and disconnected from even the most basic concepts of supply and demand—became a reality.

WE WRONGLY ALLOWED OUR PARTY TO BE ASSOCIATED WITH MCCAIN–FEINGOLD CENSORSHIP OF POLITICAL SPEECH.

The McCain–Feingold restrictions on political speech are an affront to the Constitution and a direct contradiction of the clearly stated intentions of the men who wrote it. Freedom of political speech is such a basic part of the First Amendment that some constitutional scholars have suggested it is the *only* expression that the Founders sought to protect. Yet on March 27, 2002, President Bush signed into law a measure that allows the government to outlaw certain types of political speech.

If you want to get in trouble for expressing a contrary opinion, you can go to a college campus or a Democratic cocktail party. But with McCain–Feingold, anybody can get in trouble— legal trouble—for advocating their cause or candidate. And get this—it's only illegal if you do it in order to persuade voters just before an election.

Seriously. This is the sort of nightmare George Orwell warned about decades ago.

McCain–Feingold introduced a national political speech code whose violation is punishable by a prison term. Yes, you read that right. If you want to advocate for a candidate or educate the public about an issue within a few months of an election, there are only two ways to guarantee your actions are legal. The first option is to get in line at the Federal Election Commission (FEC) to make sure your expression, formerly protected by the First Amendment, now passes muster with whomever the current unelected political appointees happen to be.

The other option guaranteed to avoid fines and keep you out of jail is to keep your mouth shut about politics and policy until it doesn't matter. That is, until an election is over.

In 2004, journalist Jonathan Rauch documented some of the first McCain–Feingold decisions by the FEC—matters formerly settled by the phrase, "It's my First Amendment right":

- In June 2004, the FEC ruled that a pro-Second-Amendment nonprofit group in Arizona could not advertise its documentary on radio or TV.
- In September 2004, the FEC prohibited a conservative filmmaker from advertising a book and a movie critical of John Kerry, the Democratic presidential nominee.
- Also that September, the FEC inserted itself into a Wisconsin race for the U.S. Senate by deciding whether a candidate's son could mention his car dealership, which was named after his father, in the dealership's ads during the election campaign.

McCain–Feingold is raw censorship, with predictably appalling results: in March 2009, a government lawyer declared before the Supreme Court that under McCain–Feingold, the government has the authority to ban corporate-funded books released before an election if they advocate for a candidate for office. The government later disavowed that statement amidst widespread condemnation of its supposed authority for book banning. But you can hardly blame it for trying—McCain–Feingold set us on the slippery slope to censorship, and the government lawyers went along for the ride.

Although most Republicans absolutely oppose this measure, a Republican president signed it into law. Democrats love this kind of political censorship, but Republicans should reject it out of hand.

Our abandonment of conservative principles had other predictable effects as well: we endured successive election defeats in 2006 and 2008, losing control of both Congress and the presidency. As a result, many of us, me included, have done some soul searching. If you don't learn from the past, you are of course destined to repeat it. This is a difficult task, but it is healthy and necessary for our party.

Now, we must quickly learn our lessons, return to our principles, and move on. We have to focus all our energy on winning the future, for time is running short. America will suffer grievously if the Obama administration succeeds in implementing its long-discredited, ultra-liberal agenda.

Republicans should unite in rejecting the core elements of this agenda: more handouts; the redistribution of wealth; diminished opportunity in the name of the latest environmental fad; the cultivation of class warfare; the undermining of personal responsibility; and the elevation of envy from character flaw to political philosophy. The Democrats' philosophy is a top-down approach that answers every problem with the creation of a new bureaucracy.

Unlike the Democrats, we have to be the party that fights for individual rights and the Constitution *as written*. To Democrats, our founding document is as pliable as silly putty. When they interpret the Constitution, they often remind me of Humpty Dumpty in that famous passage from *Through the Looking Glass*:

> "When I use a word," Humpty Dumpty said in
> rather a scornful tone, "it means just what I choose
> it to mean—neither more nor less."

Liberals sympathize with this viewpoint, because if they can make words mean anything they like, they can justify government doing anything they choose.

It's not that every liberal condescendingly believes Americans are naïve, angry rubes who need to be tamed and educated by government (notwithstanding President Obama's comment about "bitter clingers" to guns and God). It's that liberals are so convinced of their rightness and so sure of their purity of purpose that they are often unwilling to accept that words mean what they mean. To distort the meaning of words in order to justify some political goal damages our ability to agree on what government should or should not do. If the Constitution means whatever the people in power decide it means, it is unmoored from the principles that define it. The American experiment becomes a failure.

The liberal agenda is petty and unjust, but it's not difficult to sell, since it's often presented as quick-fix ideas. Do you need a job? Liberals will have the government create one for you. Are you behind on your mortgage? Today's liberals are taxing everybody else to pay it for you. Does America face enemies in the world? This liberal president is traveling around the globe to apologize and concede their arguments so they'll start liking us. And of course, if you need healthcare, liberals will have the government give it to you while magically avoiding the long waits, rationing, and stifling bureaucracy that characterize the socialized medical systems they want to emulate.

Of course, these are all shallow "solutions" that create massive new problems while only temporarily masking our existing ones. They're as practical as running an extension cord from your neighbor's house instead of paying your electric bill—and they'll work about as long and about as well.

We Republicans must present a clear alternative to the liberal agenda. We believe in free markets, free men and women, and the free exchange of ideas—and this could hardly be in greater contrast to the "we know best" attitude of liberals who are now in charge of pretty much everything. It is our task to tear the shiny wrapper off this liberal poison pill and show America what it really is.

This process has already begun, as shown by the stunning Republican victories in the November 2009 gubernatorial elections in Virginia and New Jersey. Rejecting liberal pieties outright, Robert McDonnell and Chris Christie translated conservative principles into concrete proposals to fix the problems facing their states. At a time when Americans are growing disenchanted with the neo-liberal model of fiscal recklessness, rising taxes, and overreaching government, these conservatives won not only unified Republican support, but decisive backing from independents and even from some disillusioned Democrats. Their victories point the way forward for Republican candidates: reject high-tax, high-spending liberalism—even in traditionally liberal states like New Jersey. Instead, let's try something we haven't done for a while: use conservative, fiscally responsible principles to craft solutions to our current problems. In other words, run as conservatives and then govern like conservatives.

The American people are speaking—and the Republican Party is listening. Most important, we're learning from our mistakes. With the November 2009 election of Democrat Bill Owens in New York's twenty-third congressional district, Republicans lost a long-held House seat. That race featured a battle between a liberal-leaning Republican candidate, Dede Scozzafava, and Conservative Party candidate Doug Hoffman. A groundswell of conservative opposition forced Scozzafava from the race. She then endorsed Owens, who beat Hoffman by four percentage points.

The media delighted in portraying the contest as a "civil war" within the Republican Party. It was really nothing of the kind—some conservatives believed Scozzafava was too liberal, while others simply thought she had the best chance of winning. I endorsed her before she dropped out because, as the Republican National Committee chairman, it's not my job to pontificate on which Republican candidates I like or dislike. The party's grassroots should choose the candidates, who should expect the party's support once they become our nominees.

And that was the problem in New York: Scozzafava wasn't chosen by the Republican grassroots, she was selected in a backroom deal by a handful of party chairmen. As a result, Republicans got a candidate who wasn't suited for her own district, and the grassroots rebelled. And trust me, the message of that rebellion reached the top of the party. We need to abolish the backroom wheeling and dealing and encourage all congressional districts to choose their candidates through closed primaries. By endorsing Owens, Scozzafava proved herself a disloyal Republican—such an opportunist would probably never have survived a competitive primary.

Still, the New York race was a relatively small disappointment on a night that featured the dramatic triumphs in Virginia and New Jersey. Despite Obama's victory in both those states just a year earlier, principled conservative Republicans won big, with independents swinging behind them by a decisive 2–1 margin. This bodes very well for the 2010 elections when, I expect, we will win back the New York-23 seat as part of a new Republican majority.

When people ask me why we are Republicans, I tell them it's because we believe in putting people in charge of their own lives, not putting people in line for the latest bailout scheme.

I tell them we trust the individual far more than we trust any government.

I tell them we believe in the right to run your own life as you see fit, not to do only what the government says you are fit to do.

I tell them we believe Americans have a God-given right to make their own decisions, even if some self-appointed liberal elite thinks they can choose better for you.

We believe that good ideas should succeed or fail on their merits, not on the ability of slick politicians to scare or "guilt" people into falling into line.

We believe that, as President Lincoln said, you can't fool all the people all the time—and that the delusions that this administration is peddling won't hold up to intellectually honest scrutiny.

The Republican story is one we should proclaim proudly. This party came together to help bring into reality one of the greatest ideas of the Western world: that men and women held in slavery ought to be free.

The Republican Party was founded because men of good will were compelled to do the right thing for human beings who were cruelly oppressed. These individuals knew the truth in their hearts and found it backed up by the Constitution.

How was a nation to reconcile a commitment to liberty with the evil of slavery? One of these had to go. Under the leadership of her first Republican president, Abraham Lincoln, America made the choice decisively. In doing so, she continued the effort of transforming individual freedom into a precept available to all Americans regardless of race, sex, or property ownership.

Today, it is once again only one party, the Republican Party, that is committed to individual liberty. Lincoln himself put it best when he said, "As I would not be a slave, so I would not be a master. This expresses my idea of democracy." Yet liberals, through the levers of government, now present themselves as entitled by their "wisdom" and "empathy" to be the masters of matters great and small—matters that have, until now, always been left to families and individuals and conscience.

Republicans have a duty to remind all Americans of the price paid in blood so we could all claim the great ideal—the undeniable truth—that all men are created equal, and that each has the inalienable right to conduct his or her own life as he or she sees fit—not on condition of government approval.

By reclaiming our principles, the Republican Party is again going to become the party of new ideas. In fact, this is already happening. Our governors are emerging with fresh answers to old problems, as are some of our brightest stars in Congress. Republicans are rising once again with the energy, focus, and determination to turn our timeless principles into new solutions for the future.

We must support Republican officials who assert these principles. And when they compromise on policy, we need to ensure these are tactical compromises and not departures from principle. But when elected Republicans vote against Republican principles, the voters must withhold their support—withhold it vigorously and consistently.

The responsibility of Republican voters is to elect principled Republicans and hold them accountable. Our party's accommodationism—call it "Democrat-lite Republicanism"—paved the way for the attempt at a full-blown liberal restoration we're seeing today. After all, why vote for faux Democrats when you can have the real thing in the form of Pelosi, Reid, and Obama?

Two decades after the Reagan triumph, is that really the best we can do?

Hell no.

PART

TWO

WHO WE ARE

The Obama administration's "principles" stress collectivism, group identity, and intrusive government. We should draw a sharp contrast between that agenda and our conservative principles which champion individual freedom and free markets.

STEP

3

Expose Liberal Policy as a "Reign of Error," Part I

Hitting You in the Pocketbook

AS MOST POLITICIANS will tell you, credibility and popularity are hard to build and even harder to maintain. They are also the most valuable preconditions to advancing any legislative agenda. Every new administration receives an automatic bump in public trust and popularity that translates to a kind of blank check which is valid for only a short time.

Barack Obama has tried to cash that check more times in the first year of his presidency than Americans are willing to pay. He has overstepped the bounds of responsible governance and basic accountability, and his promises of bipartisanship have been exposed as empty rhetoric papering over the same old liberal, big-government agenda.

President Obama's greatest failure so far has been his lack of trust in the American people and in the economy to which they contribute every day. His American Recovery and Reinvestment Act—the so-called "stimulus"—is not an economic repair kit but a thousand-plus page, $787 billion Democratic wish list. The president promised that all his spending and borrowing would stimulate our ailing economy and create jobs. But that's not what we got. Although the administration claimed the stimulus would keep unemployment below 8 percent, nearly a year later joblessness stands at more than 10 percent—a 26-year high. As Republicans on the Committee on Ways and Means noted, after vowing that the stimulus would create 3.5 million jobs, the Obama administration has presided over the loss of 2.7 million jobs, including job losses in forty-nine of the fifty states plus Washington, D.C.

That shouldn't be surprising. The stimulus was never really about providing jobs and relief for working families caught in hard times. The liberals used the economic crisis as an excuse to go on a reckless, wasteful, pork-laden spending spree that ushers in enormous new government interference in the private economy. Furthermore, they fomented panic, and used it to justify the government's near-takeover of the auto industry. Their intention was to re-weave the fabric of American society by further eroding what's left of the private economy.

President Obama's Chief of Staff, Rahm Emanuel, said, "You never want a serious crisis to go to waste." Now we know what he had in mind.

So far, they have gotten away with it. President Obama and the liberals have gained unprecedented and sweeping control over the economy. They are leaving the taxpayers in debt for generations and have created a ready excuse for massive tax increases in the future.

How did this happen?

By leveraging his previous popularity, and with the help of a worshipful press, President Obama portrayed traditional faith in markets as a strategy of "doing nothing." He purposefully misrepresented America's rising economic tide that has always lifted all boats—a system that has brought wealth and success to generations of Americans. By telling Americans that the economic downturn was not a brief and difficult correction but the natural state of capitalism, he tried to trick Americans into believing that free enterprise is inherently unfair, and so the government needs to take a heavier hand in running things.

The president wouldn't need Americans to believe this forever—just long enough for him to begin rewiring the economy with activist policies he knows will be difficult to untangle in the future: massive government intervention, government control, and government spending, all fueled by extravagant borrowing against the wealth of generations that haven't even been born.

President Obama and the Democrats seized the financial crisis as an opportunity to advance their agenda of establishing more federal control over all aspects of the economy. No realm is off-limits to them, and no regulation is too petty. As the *Washington Post* reported in October 2009:

> With much of Washington focused on efforts to revamp the health-care system and address climate change, a handful of Obama appointees have been quietly exercising their power over the trappings of daily life. They are awakening a vast regulatory apparatus with authority over nearly every U.S. workplace, 15,000 consumer products, and most items found in kitchen pantries and medicine cabinets.

For liberals, businesses are not the engine of American prosperity—they are harmful, greedy entities that must be constrained by the government. The Chairman of the House Financial Services Committee, Democrat Barney Frank, makes no effort to hide this ideological imperative, declaring, "We are trying in every front to increase the role of government in the regulatory area."

The Obama administration is trying to exert control, not only over how business is run, but who owns business at all. They ignore and belittle dissent, even from nonpartisan sources. They frame their arguments less often with facts than with fear-mongering to create a panicked herd mentality, and they're never above open bullying. In fact, the administration's arguments for the stimulus weren't really arguments at all, just claims that they were smarter than anybody else. They said:

- Republicans and anyone else who disagree with the administration's approach don't want to do anything at all, and you can't compromise with people who won't "play ball."
- The crisis is bearing down on us so fast that we can't afford the time to consider alternatives or even *read the entire bill.*
- All government spending can be considered a stimulus of some kind or other, so the stimulus bill is not as exceptional as it seems.
- Business owners are inherently greedy and corrupt—they are cheaters—and the only trustworthy participant is government.
- There is no need for debate because we all agree on the need for change and on the wisdom of Barack Obama.

Instead of talking about how best to spur growth—a debate between government intervention and the proven power of private enterprise—Democrats transformed their rhetoric into something much simpler to sell: *How much should we spend?* Their answer: *The more we spend, the faster the economy will improve.* Or, as Vice President Joe Biden told a bewildered AARP townhall meeting, "[W]e have to go spend money to keep from going bankrupt."

And they put our money where their mouth is. Enjoying overwhelming majorities in the House and Senate, the Democrats rammed the stimulus bill through Congress with astonishing speed. Politicians from both parties admitted they didn't have time even to read the bill. Just as disturbing, the American people were denied a meaningful debate about possible solutions. The Democrats foreclosed discussion on one of the most critical questions of the day.

Instead of an era of "change we can believe in," President Obama has ushered in a Reign of Error. Consider the arrogance, bad ideas, and poor judgment we've witnessed so far, and the president's willingness to blow up America's budget in order to finance his many boondoggles, like the pointless, $3 billion cash-for-clunkers program that mandated the destruction of perfectly functioning cars. On top of that, the future will only tell the economic damage to be wrought by the protectionist policies, the galaxy of favors to big labor, the self-destructive crusade against fossil fuels, and the new array of regulations and red tape President Obama is seeking to lasso onto American industry, all culminating with a potentially devastating cap-and-trade scheme.

I suspect if the Democratic Party actually ran on this program in 2008, the election's outcome would have been a lot different.

When the economic crisis took hold, the government stepped in with massive intervention under the Bush administration, as previously described. And President Obama has giddily continued this trajectory. The president, his appointees, and his liberal majorities in Congress have chosen at every turn to maximize federal control over banking and to eliminate or relegate to irrelevancy any discipline that is naturally imposed by the free market.

The bank bailouts gave the federal government leverage over companies that Obama doesn't want to relinquish—he has even rejected some banks' attempts to repay the bailout money. And the president's power over these institutions will vastly increase if the Senate approves the Pay for Performance Act of 2009. Already approved in the House, the bill would allow the government to dictate the salaries of all employees in any company that was bailed out.

Meanwhile, President Obama has predictably proposed a new torrent of regulation on financial firms, ostensibly to prevent a similar meltdown from happening again. These restrictions, such as forcing businesses to sell their limited banking operations and greatly increasing the regulation of hedge funds, will only distort the free market even more. They may contain unintended, unforeseen consequences just like the Community Reinvestment Act (CRA) did when it forced banks to lend money to homebuyers who didn't have the money to repay. But liberals refuse to acknowledge that. For them, our all-knowing, all-seeing government can solve every problem by the proper dose of regulation.

And to make matters worse, instead of limiting the CRA, congressional Democrats are now pushing a bill in Congress to *expand* the act by applying its lending requirements, which were previously confined to banks, to insurers, mortgage lenders, and credit unions. Liberals just don't seem to understand that it's a bad idea to force companies to loan money to people who are unlikely to pay them back. The concept is really not that complicated, but because it goes against liberal pieties about "fairness," they can't seem to wrap their heads around it.

And the worst part is this: not only do these policies damage the whole economy by destabilizing our key financial institutions, they hurt the exact people they're supposedly designed to help. You're not doing poor people a favor by getting them into a house they can't afford. Later, when they can't pay the mortgage anymore, lose their house, and have their credit ratings ruined, they'll probably wish they had bought a house they could afford in the first place.

But wait, there's more . . .

UNDER PRESIDENT OBAMA, THE GOVERNMENT HAS SEIZED THE CAR INDUSTRY.

Our government is now in the business of designing, building, manufacturing, servicing, and marketing cars.

As was the case with government intervention in the financial industry, the Bush administration opened the door to state intervention in the car industry—and the Obama administration found it needed a bigger doorway. Under President Bush, the government provided a total of $23 billion in assistance to General Motors and Chrysler at the end of 2008. The Obama administration, predictably, found this intrusion into the private sphere to be woefully inadequate. So it directly oversaw Chrysler and GM's restructuring plans, taking an 8 percent ownership stake in Chrysler and a controlling 60 percent stake in GM. The government wasn't shy about throwing its weight around either. To make sure things at GM went its way, the government fired the company's CEO. At Chrysler, when creditors protested that the restructuring program would devastate the value of their invest-ment while taking sweet care of the labor union, President Obama denounced the creditors as "speculators." White House spokesman Robert Gibbs insisted they should just be quiet and take the loss "for the greater good"—which really means "for the government's good."

Government aid to the car industry has now skyrocketed to an astounding $81 billion, most of which has gone to GM ($50 billion plus another $17 billion for its financial arm and suppli-ers). With that kind of money at stake, the government has a vested interest in making sure GM is run "correctly."

And that's the problem. Granted, GM management didn't run the company well for some time before the government takeover. (Of course, many of GM's problems stemmed from stifling government regulations and unsustainable concessions to the union—factors the Obama administration doesn't like to mention.) But at least the company was focused on making prof-itable cars.

Once the government runs a company, however, it becomes politicized. The Obama administration doesn't even hide this, announcing that car companies need to refocus on making fuel-efficient "green" cars. Whether there's actually a demand for these eco-cars, and whether they can sell profitably, is not a big concern. President Obama's overriding goal is not to make Chrysler and GM profitable, but to make them conform to his environmental vision. And if his eco-cars don't sell, well, that just creates a need for even more government intervention to prop up the companies by giving them more taxpayer money and insti-tuting new regulations that will tilt the playing field in their favor.

The Obama administration's politicized dealings with the car companies and the lack of transparency caught the attention of the Congressional Oversight Panel, which released a stinging report in September 2009. The panel criticized the Treasury Department's lack of transparency in its dealings with Chrysler and GM, recommended possibly putting the companies in a public trust to protect them from political interference, and warned that the government is unlikely to recoup billions of dollars invested in the companies.

No matter how much President Obama spins the car industry takeover as an economic benefit, it is nothing more than another government grab of private companies and another handout to the big union bosses as payback for their unquestioning support of his presidential campaign. After helping to drive Chrysler and GM into the ground, President Obama's labor buddies were rewarded in Obama's restructuring program, which effectively gave the union an 18 percent stake in GM and a 68 percent stake in Chrysler.

And what do the taxpayers get? An $81 billion bill.

Americans shouldn't be fooled. This is the real "change" President Obama has in mind for America—government ownership of our economy financed with irresponsible and reckless government spending and debt—and no jobs to show for it.

The result for the autoworkers and their families is that their financial well-being will be directly affected by an overreaching union and overbearing government.

The result for the investors and retirees who thought they were buying rock-solid GM shares is that they have ended up with worthless shares of "Government Motors."

The result for bondholders who thought they were buying the most secure investments available is that they discovered that President Obama—a former law professor—would soon override the law he once taught and upend the foundations of bankruptcy law with the stroke of a pen. His close friends, the union bosses, got their debts paid off first, and President Obama told the bondholders that their contractual investments with GM aren't worth the paper they're written on.

"Just last week, *Car and Driver* named me 'Auto Executive of the Year,'" the president joked at the 2009 White House Correspondents' Association dinner. "[It's] something I'm very proud of."

Pretty funny. But I'd feel a lot better if the president understood he's not supposed to be an auto executive. Or the head of a bank. Or the CEO of an insurance company. Or the guy who sets CEOs' salaries. Or the water-carrier for union bosses.

But wait, there's more...

UNDER PRESIDENT OBAMA OUR COUNTRY WILL, IN LESS THAN A DECADE, AMASS NEW DEBT EQUAL TO ALL THE DEBT OUR NATION HAS ACCUMULATED SINCE ITS FOUNDING.

Wondering exactly how much money Obama is spending? The Heritage Foundation explains the findings of the Office of Management and Budget's 2009 mid-session review:

Washington will spend $30,958 per household, tax $17,576 per household, and borrow $13,392 per household. The federal government will increase spending 22 percent this year to a peacetime-record 26 percent of the gross domestic product (GDP). This spending is not just temporary: President Obama would permanently keep annual spending between $5,000 and $8,000 per household higher than it had been under President George W. Bush.

Driven by this spending, America will run its first ever trillion-dollar budget deficit this year. Even worse, the President's budget would borrow an additional $9 trillion over the next decade, more than doubling the national debt. By 2019, America will be spending nearly $800 billion on net interest to service this large debt.

As the report states, "While President Obama claims to have inherited the 2009 budget deficit, it is important to note that the estimated 2009 budget deficit has increased by $400 billion since his inauguration, and the whole point of the 'stimulus' was to increase deficit spending to nearly $2 trillion based on the unproven notion that would it alleviate the recession." It further observes that the budget estimates include $1.4 trillion in tax increases, but do not include President Obama's healthcare plan which, if approved, could comprise another $1 trillion of taxes and spending.

Americans find ourselves in a severe economic crisis, with our country's finances straining under an exploding national debt. And what do we get from the Democrats? More taxes and more spending. When will they learn?

During a June 2009 interview on CNN, Minnesota governor Tim Pawlenty offered President Obama a commonsense prescription for the mess that he and the liberals are making of our economy: "With all due respect, Mr. President, if we're out of money, quit spending it."

That seems like sound advice, but the Democrats aren't listening. They're behaving like children who just came across a giant pile of candy. In fact, they're worse than that, since children would have to stop eating the candy when they ran out of it. The Democrats aren't subject to that kind of discipline. When they run out of our money, they just keep spending anyway. And it's really hard to argue that all this spending is vital to the nation. In September 2009, for example, the University of California at Santa Cruz library was awarded a federal grant worth an astounding $615,175 to upload onto the Internet its archive of the Grateful Dead, a sixties psychedelic band. While the Democrats think this is groovy, Republicans would rather see this money pay down the unprecedented debt we're foisting onto our children, or at least use it to reduce the university's tuition.

But wait, there's more . . .

WE KNOW PRESIDENT OBAMA WON'T KEEP HIS PLEDGE ONLY TO RAISE TAXES ON THE RICH— BECAUSE HE'S ALREADY BROKEN IT.

During the 2008 presidential campaign, candidate Obama promised that under his plan, "[N]o family making less than $250,000 a year will see any type of tax increase. Not your income tax, not your payroll tax, not your capital gains taxes, not any of your taxes."

That pledge didn't last long. On February 4, 2009—just fifteen days after his inauguration—Obama broke his promise by signing a bill that more than doubled federal excise taxes on cigarettes. Apparently, the president believes there are no smokers in any American family making less than $250,000 a year.

The Democrats' healthcare reform proposals also contain a slew of new taxes, though they hide these by imposing them on insurers instead of consumers. The insurers, of course, will simply pass the cost of these taxes straight down to consumers—this is how companies have historically dealt with rising taxes, regulatory fees, and other costs, and it's hard to believe liberals have somehow failed to notice it. As West Virginia Democratic senator Jay Rockefeller noted about a popular Democratic proposal to heavily tax so-called "high cost plans," it means "virtually every single coal miner is going to have a big, big tax put on them because the tax will be put on the company and the company will immediately pass it down and lower benefits."

With President Obama's healthcare plan, Americans will pay higher taxes, one way or another. So get your checks ready, and make them out to the IRS.

But wait, there's more...

PRESIDENT OBAMA WANTS TO SADDLE AMERICANS WITH THE COST OF A CAP-AND-TRADE SCHEME.

Is manmade global warming really a threat to life on earth? The answer depends on whom you ask. Many scientists insist global warming is a serious, manmade problem requiring drastic solutions. But there are other opinions you don't hear about as much. Some, such as Danish statistician Bjørn Lomborg, say manmade global warming is real but cannot be effectively countered by carbon-cutting schemes. Others, such as atmospheric physicist S. Fred Singer and former U.S. State Department agriculture analyst Dennis Avery, say the earth's increase in temperature of about one degree over the last century has nothing to do with mankind, but is part of a natural 1,500-year fluctuation pattern. And at least one scientist, climatologist Timothy Balls, claims global warming is "the greatest deception in the history of science."

In other words, there is a broad diversity of opinion about the true implications of manmade global warming, and about whether it even exists in the first place. So we should humbly acknowledge the lack of certainty in our knowledge while we continue researching the incredibly complex forces that create our climate.

But believers in catastrophic manmade global warming insist the science is beyond dispute and the debate is over. You wouldn't know that, however, by looking at the 30,000 scientists who signed the global warming petition project, which disputes the notion that manmade carbon emissions are disrupting the earth's climate.

President Obama, his liberal supporters, and congressional Democrats desperately need to convince Americans of the apocalyptic dangers of global warming—it's the key to ushering in a cap-and-trade scheme, prolonging restrictions on oil drilling, forcing the production of eco-cars, and passing countless other economically damaging environmental policies that Americans would never accept unless they believed it was a matter of life or death. Some liberals have resorted to stunning, perverse attacks on global warming skeptics. *New York Times* columnist and former Enron advisor Paul Krugman argues that doubting global warming is tantamount to committing "treason against the planet."

As always, President Obama declared his readiness to "make some tough decisions" by expanding the scope of government. The centerpiece of his plan to fight global warming is a cap-and-trade bill that would force companies to buy government-issued "permits" in order to emit carbon—the more they emit, the more they have to pay. The entire purpose is to make the use of energy sources that the president doesn't like, especially coal, rarer by making it more expensive.

The president hopes this arbitrary fee will force companies to reduce or eliminate their carbon emissions. And a few companies will probably do that. But most, especially the big power companies, will simply pass this cost to consumers by raising prices—they'll handle it the same way health insurers will cope with new taxes under the president's healthcare plan. So cap-and-trade is, in fact, another one of President Obama's disguised taxes; it will function as a *de facto* tax on energy usage by the average American household. The non-partisan Congressional Budget Office (CBO) estimated that to be effective, the cap-and-trade bill passed by the House in 2009 would have to tax the typical American family an additional $1,600 a year, and likely more.

The Obama administration publicly plays down the costs of cap-and-trade, but we now know, at least partly, what they say in private. Through a Freedom of Information Act request, the Competitive Enterprise Institute obtained Treasury Department documents estimating that President Obama's cap-and-trade plan would bring in up to $300 billion a year in new taxes on industry.

Interestingly, one document estimated the total rise in energy prices and other costs associated with cap-and-trade, but the administration censored the number before releasing the document. As CBS News blogger Declan McCullagh said, "You'd hope the presidential administration that boasts of being the 'most open and transparent in history' would be more forthcoming than this." Perhaps embarrassed by the criticism, the Treasury Department later released the censored information, which said, "While such a [cap-and-trade] program can yield environmental benefits that justify its costs, *it will raise energy prices and impose annual costs on the order of tens (and potentially hundreds) of billions of dollars.*" [emphasis added]

The president's cap-and-trade proposal differs in some ways from the cap-and-trade bill approved in the House of Representatives, and it may mutate further in the Senate. But the more we discover about the fantastic, grandiose schemes being pursued by the environmental Left, the more it seems they are not so much an attempt to "save the planet" as they are a pretext, like the economic downturn, to re-tool the economy from the ground up and replace the free market with central planning.

Liberals often falsely portray conservatives as being hostile to the environment. In reality, we all believe we have a responsibility to be good stewards of the planet, to protect this country's wondrous natural treasures, and to ensure a safe habitat for wildlife. And Americans need to discuss the facts about our environment honestly and openly, not resort to apocalyptic scare tactics and demonization. The Obama administration's environmental policies would impose crippling costs on the American economy, and we shouldn't be stampeded into adopting them.

After campaigning as a post-partisan centrist, President Obama has already pushed forward with stunning speed an ideological agenda that resurrects the failed liberal policies of the past. The broken promises and failures go on and on:

- Under President Obama, America sets a new record literally every day for being in debt to other nations.
- The president who pledged to create millions of jobs through federal public works projects now requires federal labor agreements that favor big Democrat donors, especially unions, while denying small and minority-owned businesses access to those contracts. This makes federal projects more costly, denies jobs to people who need them most, and takes money away from working families to give it to union bosses.
- Barack Obama promised to end the income tax for seniors bringing in less than $50,000 per year. When he delivered his pork-laden stimulus list, he spent hundreds of millions of taxpayer dollars on a high-priced wish list for Democratic backers, liberal pet projects, and ridiculous "green" schemes—but he couldn't make room for one thin dime of that long-promised tax cut for seniors.

- Barack Obama promised a $3,000 tax credit per worker for companies that add jobs. This measure was also missing from his stimulus and every other spending bill he passed.
- Barack Obama promised he would change the law to allow penalty-free withdrawals of up to $10,000 from 401(k) accounts. Lots of working families could use that extra money right now to pay bills or to help keep up their mortgage payments. But once in office, he didn't bother to include that benefit in his budget outline.

So what do the Democrats' economic policies mean for the mom going back to work after raising her family, or the dad who just got laid off, or the small business owner overwhelmed by the cost of just keeping the lights on? Higher taxes, fewer jobs, exploding debt, and the constant threat of inflation. President Obama is attempting to transform our economy from its reliance on the freedom and ingenuity of the private sector to command and control by Washington bureaucrats who "know best." This is his idea of "change" for our nation—and it's time we told him, "You can keep the change."

STEP

4

Expose Liberal Policy as a "Reign of Error," Part II

Taking America Down the Wrong Path

BARACK OBAMA'S "Reign of Error" is propelled by a single idea that unites his policies: he trusts government more than he trusts the American people. He and his liberal friends always insist they know best—and that they have the right to impose their choices on you.

He wants the government to take away your right to a secret ballot on whether to start a union in your workplace.

He professes respect for the Second Amendment, but supports local laws banning handgun possession. This includes the

Washington, D.C., handgun ban that was struck down by the Supreme Court in 2008.

He promises more transparency and accountability, then he expands the unaccountable bureaucracy by appointing dozens of so-called policy czars, many of whose appointments and wide authority are not subject to Senate review.

Let's take a look at a few other areas where President Obama puts the needs of big government ahead of your own. Perhaps nothing demonstrates this tendency more than his unsparing efforts to "reform" healthcare—a move that would put a bureaucrat in charge of your healthcare, limit your choice of doctors, and encourage your employer to cancel your current insurance.

American healthcare needs reform—Democrats and Republicans agree on that much. But that's where the agreement ends.

Republican thinking on healthcare is straightforward: fix the parts of the system that are failing, strengthen what already works, and above all, *do no harm.* There are two big steps we could take immediately that wouldn't cost taxpayers a dime. First, enact comprehensive tort reform to stamp out the practice of defensive medicine and to keep doctors from fleeing states where frivolous lawsuits have driven up the cost of their insurance premiums. Second, allow the cross-state sale of insurance premiums to stimulate competition among insurers.

Democrats, in contrast, have a hidden agenda. They want to replace America's system of private insurance with a massive scheme for socialized medicine run by government bureaucrats. A few Democrats will tell you that's their real goal, but not many, and certainly not President Obama. Instead, they put forward their plans under the pleasant-sounding euphemism of "reform." But their plans are much more ambitious than that—and you don't have to take my word for it. Just look at what the president and his liberal allies are proposing.

The Democrats' goal for years has been to approve the so-called "public option" for insurance. It will be a brand-new, government-run insurance system that will compete with private insurers. The pitch is simple: if you are an employer or a private citizen and you don't want private insurance, you can go with government coverage instead. At first glance, that seems harmless (it always does), and it might even sound like a pretty good idea. It's presented as a way to increase competition by introducing a new, optional choice.

But it won't boost competition, and it won't stay optional for long. Here's why: the government has an overwhelming advantage over any ordinary business. Unlike private companies, the new government insurance company will not have to make any money. (Think of Amtrak or the post office, for example.) It can spend whatever it likes and make up the difference with more taxes and more borrowing.

That means the price of the government's premiums doesn't have to reflect the true cost of healthcare. The government can set the price arbitrarily low, which is what it would do. What would be the point of this "public option" if its premiums weren't cheaper than those you can already buy from the private sector? Now, Democrats argue this government program could cover people who are denied coverage by private insurers—people who typically have pre-existing conditions or otherwise require very expensive care. Fair enough. But President Obama also vows the program will be self-sustaining, paying for itself solely through the premiums it collects.

And that's impossible. The only way the government could afford to cover *everyone* who applies would be by using taxpayer funds. The ability to offer below-cost premiums and to cover the most expensive care regardless of cost would give the government an insurmountable advantage over private companies which, of course, don't have access to an endless supply of taxpayer money.

So the "public option" won't be subject to pesky limitations like the competitive marketplace. It will always be the lowest-price option, because its costs will simply be passed along to the whole country through taxes, fees, and yet more massive federal borrowing, which will rack up even more debt for our kids and grandkids.

Unable to compete, private insurance will be driven out of business. The "public option" will become the only option you have. Some liberals acknowledge this openly. Speaking about Hillary Clinton's and Barack Obama's healthcare plans during the Democratic primaries, *New York Times* columnist Paul Krugman told an interviewer their plans "build on the existing private insurance system, but crucially they also allow people to buy into a publicly run plan, which would compete and, I believe, actually would in the end kill the private plans in the competition." And Obama, of course, has been caught on tape advocating a "single payer universal healthcare plan," which is a euphemism for government-run healthcare.

We've seen the "public option" before, in a different area. In 1993, the Democratic Congress created the Ford Direct

Loan Program, which was pitched as a "public option" for student loans. The idea was that the government would directly provide student loans, in addition to giving guarantees and subsidies for private lenders as it had been doing. This was meant to increase competition in the student loan market—the same argument the Democrats make now for the public option in healthcare. But competition suddenly become irrelevant in September 2009, when the Democratic House of Representatives, with President Obama's support, passed a bill mandating that the government directly take over the guaranteed private loans, pushing the private lenders out of the market. If the bill passes the Senate and President Obama signs it, the public option will become the only option.

Once we have government-run healthcare, there is no telling what trajectory it will take. Maybe it will be like England where, according to the *Daily Telegraph*, a group of medical experts recently warned of a spreading "'tick box' culture" where healthcare staff are effectively euthanizing patients who might not actually be dying. Or it might be like Canada, where government healthcare is so inefficient that citizens routinely come to America to avoid waiting months or even years for surgeries. (It's unclear where those Canadians would go if America adopted a system like the one from which they're fleeing.) As for customer service, well, if you like your experience at the Department of Motor Vehicles, you will *love* government-run healthcare!

Alongside the public option, we find a ream of Democratic proposals for more regulation and more government mandates. These include a government-run "healthcare exchange" that would favor insurers who consent to more regulation; the "employer mandate," which would force employers to cover their employees' health insurance; and the "individual mandate," which would force *all* Americans to buy health insurance whether they want it or not. As for that last measure, President Obama's belief that the Constitution allows the government to fine, imprison, or otherwise punish every American who doesn't buy health insurance tells us all we need to know about his views on individual rights.

All these proposals reflect the same mentality that big government works better than the free market. The notion is not even considered that existing regulations, like those preventing insurers from competing across state lines, create a lot of the current problems, and that the answer might be more free competition, not a massive bureaucratic program to plan and manage the entire healthcare sector.

And how much will all this cost? President Obama conjured the figure of $900 billion for his entire plan over ten years. Another near-trillion dollar spending program would be bad enough, but this figure isn't even credible. It assumes hundreds of billions of dollars in saving by eliminating waste and abuse in the current system. That Obama can help fund his program by saving this fantastic amount of money, which conveniently does not require spending cuts or any new taxpayer spending, is truly miraculous. As Charles Krauthammer remarked, "That's not a lie. That's not even deception. That's just an insult to our intelligence."

President Obama has not come clean with the American people about his healthcare plan. He says employer-provided policies will be secure, but he wants to allow companies to pay a fee and then dump their employees into the public option. He says the plan won't add to the deficit, but it will explode the deficit.

He champions bipartisanship, but he supports a process where Nancy Pelosi rams a 2,000-page healthcare bill through the House of Representatives on a Saturday night with just a single Republican vote.

Obama vehemently denies he's trying to build an entirely new healthcare system. Well, Dr. Frankenstein didn't think he was building a monster, either. But that's exactly what the president is doing.

One thing is for sure: the further the government becomes involved in healthcare, the more it will want to get involved even deeper. Because that's how every bureaucracy behaves—it seeks to expand its authority. Consider this: if government pays your healthcare bills, it will have a vested interest in regulating your health. And the most direct approach to keeping you "healthy"— as the government defines it—would be to ration your care. Unless you take care of your health as the government dictates— if you don't lose weight, or quit smoking, or exercise enough, or stop eating fast food—there could be consequences. After all, the bureaucrats will say, why should you get the very best treatment for your heart disease if you won't take the time to lose those extra twenty pounds? That wouldn't be *fair*.

Liberals, or course, swear up and down this isn't what they want. But it sure would be consistent with their growing conviction that the government needs to force Americans to live "healthier" lifestyles. Liberal-run cities across the nation are already banning restaurants from using what they deem "unhealthy" ingredients. And there is now a growing demand among liberals to discourage you from consuming "unhealthy" foods and soft drinks by slapping new "sin taxes" on them. New York Democratic governor David Paterson gave up his plan for an 18 percent tax on soft drinks amidst a public uproar, but that hasn't stopped President Obama from floating a similar idea for a *federal* tax on sugary drinks. The president remarked, "Look, people's attitude is that they don't necessarily want Big Brother telling them what to eat or drink, and I understand that. It is true, though, that if you wanted to make a big impact on people's health in this country, reducing things like soda consumption would be helpful."

This statement is a classic liberal justification for intrusive government. I know you don't want the government telling you what to eat, what to drink, and how to live, Obama is saying, but your health is far too important to be left in your own hands. You might make the wrong decisions. You might drink too many soft drinks. So the government needs to slap you with a tax penalty to encourage you to decide these matters the way it thinks you should decide them.

And all this is *before* government has direct responsibility for paying your healthcare bills. Americans are already tired of intrusive government, but Barack Obama's socialized medicine is a prescription for the most invasive nanny state imaginable.

Let me reiterate: America needs healthcare reform. Prices are already too high, and they are rapidly climbing higher. The uninsured need better access to healthcare. Insurance needs to become more available to people with pre-existing conditions. And we all deserve to know we won't be kicked out—or priced out—of the policies we already have.

Yet the Democrats' answer is to gradually usher in a government-run system, thus junking every part of a healthcare system that covers five-sixths of our population! (And of the 46 million uninsured, keep in mind that 9.7 million are not American citizens; 17.6 million make over $50,000 a year; and another 14 million are already eligible for Medicade and SCHIP.) When your plumber says you need a new faucet or a new drain, do you replace every pipe in the house? Of course not. But that's what the Democrats are trying to do with healthcare.

By the way, I'm not asking you to feel sorry for the insurance companies. Republicans are working for healthcare reform that demands insurance companies treat people a lot more fairly. But the choice isn't whether or not to deal with an insurance company; it's whether to deal with a private insurance company or a government bureaucrat in Washington, D.C.

At least you have some leverage over your insurance company. If you're mistreated, you can typically appeal decisions to arbitrators. Employees can encourage their employer to switch policies, and some people can simply switch insurers on their own. But when Washington runs the system, the bureaucrat on the other end of the phone owes you *nothing*. You can't even threaten to take your business elsewhere. ObamaCare will be the only game in town.

In reality, the Democrats don't have a healthcare plan so much as a scheme to shift the cost of healthcare to our children and grandchildren. It's a risky, arrogant, and disingenuous demolition of a good, though imperfect, system, and Republicans are going to continue exposing it. We will fight for reforms that put power in the hands of patients, not bureaucrats appointed by the Obama administration.

PRESIDENT OBAMA HAS POLITICIZED THE U.S. CENSUS.

"It's not the voting that's democracy, it's the counting."

That's a line from a play by Tom Stoppard, and it nicely sums up the win-at-all-costs approach of so many Democrats.

Democrats were despondent when they came up short in the close presidential elections of 2000 and 2004. Who wouldn't be? But instead of putting our differences aside and working to reunite the country, they committed their energies to trying to undermine President Bush's authority. They polarized the nation by demonizing duly-elected administrators such as attorneys general Katherine Harris in Florida and Ken Blackwell in Ohio, accusing them of "stealing" elections when they simply carried out their official responsibilities. To compound the impact, they cast doubt on the voting system itself, even spreading crazy conspiracy theories about "rigged" voting machines and shadowy corporate villains who could magically fix vote totals for everything from the presidency all the way down to dog catcher.

At times, their campaign to undermine elections went beyond fear-mongering to the tacit endorsement of physical intimidation—the kind Democrats and Republicans stood against together only a generation ago. When members of the New Black Panther Party intimidated voters at poll entrances in

Philadelphia on Election Day 2008, the liberal press mostly laughed off the story, if they covered it at all. The press used to regard voter intimidation as a crucial civil rights issue— apparently not anymore. And, as mentioned earlier, Barack Obama's Department of Justice ordered the prosecution of these Panthers to be dropped.

Three months before that, President Obama's attorney general, Eric Holder, gave a now-infamous speech declaring that America is "a nation of cowards" when it comes to discussing matters of race. This is a vicious insult in itself, but when it comes from an individual who shuts down an investigation of voter intimidation for obvious political reasons, it is despicable. Attorney General Holder is sworn to uphold equal justice under the law. Let's hope that during his tenure, none of his political opponents will need to rely on him for justice.

Of course, when the Democrats won big in the 2008 elections, they immediately ceased all their jeremiads against the voting system—suddenly it worked just fine. Funny how there only seem to be problems when Republicans win.

After spending most of a decade undermining public confidence in our election system, the Democrats recently tried to game that very system by securing behind-the-scenes jobs for thousands of unscrupulous leftwing activists in conducting the 2010 U.S. Census.

It's important to understand that the census isn't just a head count for the record books. The data are used to determine how government money is distributed and, most important, how congressional and legislative districts are apportioned. Because there's a lot riding on the census, it's crucial that the public have confidence in its accuracy and fairness. If one party could gain partisan influence over the census, it could easily change a few numbers here and there to increase its representation in state capitols and in Congress.

The Democrats have tried to manipulate the census before. In 2000, they quietly encouraged activist groups to challenge the census in an effort to replace its strict head count with sampling and computer-generated "estimates"—a back-door way to inflate the number of people associated with traditional liberal constituencies. Not only would such sampling have been fundamentally unfair, it would also have been blatantly illegal: in 1999, the Supreme Court ruled that sampling could not be used to apportion congressional seats. Not that this stopped the Democrats from trying.

With the 2010 census approaching, the Democrats reverted to their old tricks. The tip of their sword this time was supposed to be the Association of Community Organizers for Reform Now. ACORN, as it is better known, is a radical leftwing activist organization. It is perhaps best known for the many accusations of voter fraud leveled against its members in the 2006 and 2008 elections. The potentially criminal activities of ACORN members have brought arrests, indictments, police raids, and formal investigations throughout the country. The group made headlines in September 2009, when Florida authorities issued arrest warrants for eleven ACORN members suspected of falsifying hundreds of voter registration cards during the 2008 elections.

But thanks to former "community organizer" Barack Obama, the community organizers at ACORN were appointed as official "national partners" in the 2010 census, entrusted with recruiting some of the workers who will actually conduct the head count. Despite public outrage, a corrupt, partisan group that specializes in voter fraud was set to help conduct the census.

But then, disaster struck ACORN—undercover filmmakers posing as a pimp and a prostitute recorded employees from multiple ACORN offices advising them on how to establish a brothel, claim illegal benefits for underage prostitutes, falsify tax forms, smuggle illegal aliens into America, and lie to police officers. ACORN's sordid history of corruption did not disqualify it from participating in the census, but the prostitution exposé was just too much. Soon afterward ACORN was ejected from the census, and Congress voted to cut off the group's government funding to boot.

The Democrats' attitude is this: if the rules don't produce the "correct" political outcome, grab power and make new rules. That happens to be ACORN's *modus operandi* as well. In just such an effort, President Obama announced in February 2009 his intention to remove the census from its traditional oversight by the Commerce Department and make it a White House function overseen by a political appointee. This was a shocking power grab unprecedented in the census's history.

It should come as no surprise that President Obama and ACORN were cooperating closely on their census project, since Obama has a history with those types of dubious organizations. When he appeared at a 2007 presidential candidates' forum sponsored by ACORN and other "community organizer" groups, the moderator asked if a delegation from the groups could meet with him in his first hundred days in office. Obama couldn't throw open the Oval Office fast enough: "Yes! But let me even say before I even get inaugurated, during the transition we're going to be calling all of you in to help us shape the agenda. We're going to be having meetings all across the country with community organizations so that you have input into the agenda for the next presidency of the United States of America."

That explains at least some of the strange ideas coming out of this White House. The radicals have a key to the front door— and a fellow "community organizer" on the inside who shares their agenda.

PRESIDENT OBAMA SUPPORTS PRIVATE EDUCATION—FOR HIS OWN KIDS.

I can't honestly say that President Obama *always* prefers big government. After looking long and hard, I found a government program he eliminated. Despite his willingness to spend close to $800 billion to "stimulate" all sorts of ridiculous enterprises and wasteful schemes, the president could not tolerate a modest, local program that helped poor families send their kids to good private schools.

Like all good parents, President Obama wants the best education for his children. Fortunately, he can afford it. He sends his daughters to Sidwell Friends, known as the "Harvard of Washington's private schools," where tuition is about $30,000 a year per child.

Why doesn't he send them to public school? That's easy. According to *Education Week* magazine's most recent "Quality

Counts" report, Washington, D.C., public schools earned a D+ rating—making them the absolute worst in the nation.

For a while, there was a little hope for D.C. parents. Under the D.C. Opportunity Scholarship program, the low-income parents of 1,700 D.C. children received vouchers to get their kids out of D.C.'s disastrous public schools and into private schools of their choice. But in spring 2009, President Obama approved a spending bill that killed the program. He thus slammed the door of opportunity shut on some of America's neediest and most vulnerable young people.

Of course, the Democrats can say they didn't want it to end this way, and they didn't. But don't think that means they were sympathetic to these kids. Their original plan for ending the program was even harsher. They first proposed shutting the program immediately and pulling the scholarships from the current roster of 1,700 kids who had already been awarded them. Letting these kids stay in school to graduate while "only" cutting off all future scholarship recipients was the Democrats' idea of a generous compromise.

President Obama and his liberal allies cynically tried to cover their tracks. Democratic senator Dick Durbin inserted some clever language in a spending bill so that if Congress did nothing, the kids' scholarships would simply expire. That way, the Democrats wouldn't have to go on record casting a vote to eliminate scholarships for poor children. As Bill McGurn put it in the *Wall Street Journal*, it was "[j]ust the sort of sneaky maneuver that's so handy when you don't want inner-city moms and dads to catch on that you are cutting one of their lifelines."

Democratic congressmen, senators, and even presidents proclaim the virtues of public education and oppose vouchers and private schools, but you'll notice that when the public schools are a wreck, they're the first ones to abandon ship. Here in D.C., President Obama doesn't have a problem cutting off the lifeline for kids who need a good education as much or more than any children in the nation. After all, he can afford to send his kids to Sidwell Friends, and he needs to keep the teachers' union bosses happy. He won't sacrifice his own kids for the teachers' unions— and he shouldn't. But he shouldn't sacrifice other people's kids, either. Once again, Bill McGurn hits the nail on the head:

> [I]t points to perhaps the most odious of double standards in American life today: the way some of our loudest champions of public education vote to keep other people's children—mostly inner-city blacks and Latinos—trapped in schools where they'd never let their own kids set foot. This double standard is largely unchallenged by either the teachers' unions or the press corps. For the teachers' unions, it's a fairly cold-blooded calculation. They're willing to look the other way at lawmakers who chose private or parochial schools for their own kids—so long as these lawmakers vote in ways that keep the union grip on the public schools intact and an escape hatch like vouchers bolted.

Vice President Biden's grandchildren attend Sidwell. Bill Clinton's daughter went there too, and so did Al Gore's son. President Obama is just carrying on a hypocritical Democrat tradition that boils down to this: do as I say, not as I do.

Inventory Our Principles

WE ARRIVE at our moral and political principles through self-examination, through our experiences with our families and communities, and through the study of history. We conserve what is best—hence the word "conservative"—and seek patterns so we might learn what truly makes something good or valuable. But where do we first learn how to live a dignified life and what really matters in the world?

I learned this from a sharecropper's daughter. Her folks had to pull her out of school in the fifth grade to work in the cotton fields of South Carolina. She worked her whole life to provide for her family, never making more than minimum wage.

That woman is my mother, Maebell.

Through the remarkable example of her life, her will, and her experiences, my mother taught me the value of self-discipline and self-reliance matched with compassion for those in need. She said that one of the best ways to meet your obligation to others is to live life as if everybody were watching what you do or say.

She taught me to know God, to respect others and myself, and to keep that "pecking order" in mind in all things. Cultivating this mindset of respect for self, generosity of spirit, love for God, and caring for others is, to me, the real American dream.

But as I look around today, I see many people setting aside that dream for a false promise.

While hard work and careful planning often lead to material wealth, there is a growing perception that we are naturally entitled to prosperity regardless of our effort, and that fabulous wealth is far more common than it really is. What's worse, many people—especially our young—now believe the heartbreaking lie that money, power, fame, and material things are the keys to a happy life.

But money is not a cure-all, power does not bring satisfaction, fame is not noble, and material things cannot fill the God-shaped hole in the human heart.

For many folks—and believe me, I know the temptation—life's priorities are out of whack. But the answer isn't simply to show that poor choices have poor consequences. We must help people understand that they have the right to choose how to live their own lives, and that good choices can have great consequences not only for themselves, but also for their family, community, and nation.

As Republicans, our first job ought to be setting that example in our own lives. I learned it by watching my mother live that way every day. Come to think of it, she always had two jobs: doing whatever it was she had to do—picking cotton, washing laundry, or being a wife and mother—and providing an example for my sister, me, and anyone else who happened to notice.

Maebell has not lived a life of ease and comfort, but for her it still has been the American dream: to live by her own choices—her own hope and heart—and to hold herself to a high and noble standard. Ask her if she has lived a good life. She will tell you her answer before you get the question out of your mouth: *Yes, baby.*

People who want to live life with hope and heart must remember that the American dream is not possessions, rewards, or recognitions, but a life of seeking both opportunity and service. The American dream is a life well-lived.

And the best news of all about the American dream is this: it is available to anyone willing to claim it. It is a legacy to which everyone has a right. Your name doesn't have to be Rockefeller or Vanderbilt or even Oprah to stake your claim.

That dream has taken me on a long and wonderful journey from seeing my mother leave home every morning for hand work at the laundry, to watching her smile as I took the oath of office to become lieutenant governor of the state of Maryland and then the first African-American chairman of the Republican National Committee. As the son of an abusive, alcoholic father, that dream led me from the childhood terror of seeing my father hurting my mother, to being a proud father of my own children and sharing every day of life with a loving, caring, and beautiful wife. And as an African-American, I proudly see that dream has led black people from historic, institutional oppression, to opportunity across the spectrum of culture and economics, and to a life of success and true happiness for a man like me.

People ask me, "How did all this happen for you?"

I always tell 'em the same thing: it was Maebell.

Maebell raised me to understand and appreciate some enduring principles:

- You cannot bring about prosperity by discouraging thrift.
- You cannot strengthen the weak by weakening the strong.
- You cannot help the wage earner by pulling down the wage payer.
- You cannot further the brotherhood of man by encouraging class hatred.
- You cannot help the poor by destroying the rich.
- You cannot build character and courage by taking away man's initiative and incentive.
- You cannot help men in the long run by doing for them what they should do for themselves.

Maebell didn't make these up herself—these principles have been attributed to various people, including President Lincoln.

And to me, they are a whole lot more than Mother's smart advice. They help make me who I am—and, when I stumble, they remind me of the man I want to be.

But what is the ultimate source of those principles? From what fundamental idea do they flow? Read through them again, and I think their foundation will become clear. They recognize the obligation we have to others. They reject the casting of blame. They call for elevation of self, not the denigration of others. Overall, they call for us to reach for something better within ourselves, not to drag down the best in others in the name of parity. What's more, if you think about each of these things, everyday experience tells you they work. Therefore, I believe our principles must have two simple but profound qualities, one that prescribes their purpose and another that prescribes their execution: our principles must promote freedom, and they must inspire action.

Freedom, by definition, is the right to conduct our lives as we see fit. It is the most basic human right, and it is a *natural right*— that is, it belongs to us by virtue of our birth as human beings, not as citizens of some country or adherents of some ideology, and not because it has been granted to us by a person, group, or government. In other words, every human being in every nation is born with the right to be free. That does not mean we all get to exercise that right, because not all of us are citizens of a nation that protects the right to freedom. But freedom will always be non-negotiable and the greatest "good" thing that exists.

Long before "Live free or die" became the motto of New Hampshire, General John Stark declared it in 1809 in a letter to fellow veterans of the American Revolution. It resonates with

Americans in general and with Republicans in particular because it is such a clear distillation of America's founding idea. Note that General Stark didn't say, "Live sort of free," or "I'd gladly trade living free for some 'free' healthcare and a retirement package and a government-managed economy."

Yet two hundred years later a whole lot of Americans are happy to trade little pieces of freedom for what they think is greater security—conceding parts of their economic liberty, their physical safety, and more. And as Benjamin Franklin wrote a generation before the founding, "Those who sacrifice liberty for security deserve neither."

At a time when many Americans are compromising their freedom, Republican principles must promote it. No political party can claim a stronger commitment to freedom and liberty than the Republican Party—we are the Party of Lincoln.

When women and men were bound in chains, it was the Republican Party that took action to end slavery. Our forebears carried out this profoundly moral act because it was the right thing to do. It was a devastating political choice, but political expediencies should never—and in this case did not—keep us from doing what's right.

And when we do what's right, we gain sincere, long-term supporters. But let's be clear, I'm talking about principled acts, not pandering and empty promises. The Republican Party didn't come about because a handful of individuals in the 1850s put forward a laundry list of pet programs. If they had, they could have taken their ideas to the Democrats, the Whigs, the Liberty Party, the Free Soil Party, or the Know-Nothings. They were willing to disagree among themselves on tactics, but as committed opponents of slavery, they were without a home, so they organized a party based on that principle. That way, like-minded citizens could stand together and have a voice in shaping the future of the young nation.

This principle-driven identity is what the Republican Party has lost and what we now must regain.

As Republicans, we can disagree among ourselves on how best to put principles into action. Such disagreement is good and necessary, because debate, discussion, and advocacy are how we improve policy. But any principle we embrace must form the foundation for debate, not become the topic of debate. We must hold the principle in common, it must be grounded in freedom, and it must lead to effective policy.

But what should that principle be? Does one stand out more than others? Yes it does: individual rights. The fight for individual rights is what brought our nation into existence and gave root to our party one hundred years later. It is the foundation of Western civilization, and a pure expression of absolute respect for human dignity. It is, above all else, the principle to which the Republican Party must return.

The other quality that our principles must have is "action," and by this I mean that we must act on what we propose, our proposals must be effective, and they must work the way we say they will. This may sound obvious, but for many politicians and special interests, whether something actually works is often an afterthought. Many of them only want to win—for themselves, their cause, their group, or their personal opinions.

As Republicans, we must do better. It is not enough to advocate some plan because it reflects an ideology we like. Democrats do that, and look what it's doing to our freedoms. If we advocate an idea, it must not be enough for us to think it sounds "conservative." We need to know, and not simply hope, that it's going to do what we promise when it's put into practice.

To borrow a famous phrase, the "audacity of hope" can inspire, but without the work to back it up, "hope" never created anything—never put a roof over someone's head, never helped someone find a job, never fed a hungry family, never made a man or woman free. A fellow may hope that he will fly when he jumps off a mountain, but gravity doesn't care about hope. Pretty words won't make you fly, and audacity won't save you from a crushing fall.

The "hope" so many talk about now isn't much more than hero worship. These days, "hope" means an empty promise that all your wishes will come true. Remember the news stories in the 2008 election campaign about people who believed that Obama would pay their gas bills and make our enemies into friends just by shaking hands? Since those heady days, the bloom has come off that rose, thankfully.

Real hope is an informed confidence rooted in history, experience, and knowledge. Man has known this for centuries. St. Paul identified it in the Bible when he described faith not as blind optimism, but as the evidence of things not seen. Another generation is about to learn that hard lesson for itself.

Conservatives don't need to reinvent that wheel. One of the reasons conservatism succeeds is its respect for history and the real world. We look for guidance from what has been proven over time. Thousands of years of recorded human experience provide an awesome record of what works and what doesn't. It's a practical guide to achieving real change by saving us the wasted effort of reinventing success or repeating failure.

People have inherent value. We matter because we *are*. And no government authority is entitled to tell a person how he must run his life. To do so would deny that person some measure of his worth and infringe on his individual rights. As the founders wrote, we hold these truths to be self-evident.

At the same time, we accept some constraints on individual rights because we want to maintain a society in which we can appropriately exercise those rights. The benefits of civil society outweigh the burdens of limiting our rights as long as the limits are reasonable. How and whether to expand such limits is the essence of politics: we seek consensus on the balance between individual rights and an ordered society.

Republicans recognize that in order to protect individual rights, people must accept limits on those rights only to the extent necessary to ensure order. Government should be the vehicle to aid "we the people" in establishing a more perfect union—at least that was the original intention. But as with so many good intentions, leaders become obsessed with the power of government at the expense of the rights of individuals. Think of all the ways that government at every level has come to infringe on your rights because those in charge cannot resist wielding their power. Every day, government promotes some cause or agenda only because someone with authority deems it "worthwhile"—though usually under the cover of an ever-expanding definition of what is "necessary" for society.

Think about the rise of political correctness. It started as a posture among liberal academics, then evolved into enforceable speech codes at universities, then grew into "hate crime" laws that increase a punishment because of the *attitude* of the criminal toward his victim. Political correctness evolved from a personal viewpoint held by a few people into a growing list of criminalized opinions that the state may prosecute under penalty of law. And the Obama administration seems intent on dramatically expanding the realm of thought crimes. In addition to approving yet another new hate crimes law, the Obama administration—oblivious to the threat to free speech—cosponsored a resolution approved by the UN Human Rights Council that commits governments to combat various types of hate speech, incitement, and "stereotyping"—a resolution that is extremely difficult to square with the First Amendment.

Are racism, sexism, and other prejudicial attitudes bad things? Of course. But what will we do as powerful officials, lawmakers, and judges begin punishing more opinions according to their own prejudices? We may detest what someone else says or thinks, but the minute we start criminalizing opinions, no matter how unpleasant they are, we surrender our individual rights—and who knows if our opinions will be next? Think about that the next time you take an unpopular moral stand—or the next time you think "there oughta be a law" when someone expresses an opinion *you* dislike.

Not only is government gaining a veto over unpopular opinions, it recently declared its right to decide which businesses fail and which survive. Historically, a business that can't stay in business goes out of business. It is usually replaced by a new enterprise that has a more efficient business model, or that provides other goods or services that the public wants. Lost jobs return as part of a new business that better serves the public. The profits from increased efficiency get invested to create other new businesses, expand existing ones, raise salaries, or buy other goods and services. This is Free Enterprise 101.

Consider once again the fate of Chrysler and General Motors. In 2008 and 2009, the companies found they no longer produced the kinds of cars that Americans wanted to buy. This happens in industries all the time: car companies themselves once made history of horse-buggy makers. A handful of computer manufacturers overwhelmed IBM. Microsoft's word processing software buried the typewriter business. Build a better mousetrap and the world will beat a path to your door—or fail to sell what the public wants and watch them go somewhere else.

In 2009, liberals swept the rules aside and engineered the government takeover of both auto firms. Think about the overall principle: the government simply didn't care that people had shown, through their purchases, that they preferred other car companies and other types of cars. Liberals decided that the public might know what it wants, but the government knows what we *need*—what car companies we need to stay in business and what kinds of cars we need them to make.

It was a sickening display of disregard for the American people, American history, and the proper limits of government.

There was a time when even children understood that the government is not supposed to pick winners and losers in business—

or in religion, your personal life, or anything else. So why doesn't the President of the United States know that?

Here's a remedial civics lessons for President Obama: the government is supposed to maintain a level playing field for everybody, not move the goal posts closer to one team or another according to government preferences. When the government picks winners and losers, businesses spend more time sucking up to government and less time improving their products and services. Businesses should prosper or fail based on their own competency, not on their ability to curry favor with the powerful.

We need to defend individual rights in order to limit government power. Government's natural tendency is always to grow, justifying new programs through an ever-expanding definition of what is necessary for society. Call it "government by whim"—and look where it's leading.

The government already tells us how much water our toilets can flush and what kind of light bulbs we can buy—for our own good, it says. A friend of mine in Fairfax County, Virginia, can't install a new staircase rail in his own home because it isn't "wheelchair-friendly"—never mind that no one in his house uses a wheelchair, and never mind that he owns the house. The same government that "gives" you bicycle paths and museums is always finding more expansive ways to define what is "for the good of the community."

And these proposals for never-ending nanny state regulations are getting more intrusive and more invasive every day. Alabama officials have proposed a fat tax on overweight city employees;

California regulators sought to ban the sale of dark colored cars; also in the Sunshine State, the California Energy Commission lobbied to require private homes to use special thermostats that allow the utility company to control your home temperature. Every time one of these outrageous proposals is rejected (usually after receiving some unexpected and unwelcome publicity), two new ones pop up to replace it.

When it seemed we were getting something for nothing, we didn't speak out. Who doesn't want some new civic bauble paid for by someone else? But all this paved the way for what's happening today. Washington has gone from protecting our individual rights to granting us ever more limited permission to exercise them.

President Gerald Ford put it best when he said, "A government big enough to give you everything you want is strong enough to take everything you have." I fear that Americans don't take that to heart. In a recent Rasmussen survey, a mere 53 percent of Americans agreed that capitalism is better than socialism, so we may be a lot closer than we realize to surrendering our rights for good, one little bit at a time—and that's a scary thought.

It's time for Republicans to articulate our principles. Let us once again stand for individual rights as the foundation of freedom and real liberty. We should remind people what we stand to lose at the hands of an ever-encroaching government. And let's also declare what we can gain from freedom and individual liberty: we can keep more of what we earn; we can better afford to educate our children and have more choices about what kind of education they will receive; we can cultivate a healthier economy with more jobs; and we can choose our healthcare program instead of lining up for a government-run "one-size-fits-all" system.

When the government's reach is limited by the will of the people, we can have the environment cared for by local conservationists instead of ideological extremists who don't care about preserving local jobs and communities. We can reduce the harm and divisiveness of political correctness by removing its legal sanction. We can limit the power of "empathetic" judges who disrespect the rule of law. We can expand school choice, exposing the hypocrites who extol the wonders of public education while sending their own kids to private school. (Are you listening, President Obama?) And we can truly help those in need by keeping a safety net for the most disadvantaged, while reducing ineffective government handouts and encouraging more targeted, efficient assistance by local organizations, communities, churches, and private charities.

It is time for America to part ways with liberal groupthink, hypocrisy, and hero worship. It is time for Republicans to return to our founding principle: the protection of individual rights, leading to liberty and justice for all.

6

Contrast Our Principles with Theirs, Part I

Identity Politics and Judicial Activism

LIBERALISM doesn't work—but you don't have to take my word for it. Just read a little history. The liberals' "War on Poverty," begun in 1964, helped lock in a poverty rate that hasn't budged since the 1970s. Liberals have expanded Social Security from a Depression-era retirement program into a mammoth, catch-all public insurance system headed for bankruptcy. The liberal insistence on telling entrepreneurs how to run their businesses has resulted in burdensome regulations that wrack up an estimated *trillion dollars* in annual compliance costs, according to economist Mark Crain.

Those are a few of the bigger cases of liberal failure, and there are nearly limitless additional examples: multi-billion-dollar government bureaucracies that achieve nothing; environmental rules that cut jobs instead of pollution; school programs that subvert parental choice (not to mention the actual education of children); and public safety campaigns that hold more benefits for criminals than for law-abiding citizens.

How do modern liberals come up with so many policies that inflict so many bad things on so many good people? Well, policy flows from principle, and it is becoming increasingly clear that liberals have turned away from a principled commitment to the rights of the individual.

Liberals and conservatives used to be united in this commitment, but those days are gone. You can see it in liberal proposals, and you can hear it in the way liberals talk. It's always about the need for government to give an advantage to one class of people over another—"poor" versus "rich" or the "haves" versus the "have-nots"—and how some group has gotten ahead at the expense of another. I mentioned earlier how liberals are picking winners and losers in corporate America. Well, the Left does the same thing with different categories of people. But what they do is even worse than just moving the goalposts; instead of maintaining a level playing field, they try to remove groups they don't like from the field altogether.

Thus, the core difference between liberalism and conservatism today can be summed up as a difference of values:

Liberals believe the most important unit of society is the *community*.

Conservatives believe the most important unit of society is the *individual*.

This difference is expressed in policies: liberal policies aim to help individuals by helping some larger group to which they supposedly belong; conservatives, in contrast, want to help individuals by removing obstacles that prevent them from advancing through their own integrity and hard work.

Liberals instinctively seek to use the coercive power of government to force *their* choices on *you*. Sometimes it's in a big way, as with the Obama administration's attempt to compel all Americans, through force of law, to buy health insurance. And sometimes it's in a small way, as when Congress mandated how much ethanol must be added to your gasoline.

Consider smoking bans. They're a minor inconvenience for some and a welcome development for many others who find smoking to be unhealthy, unpleasant, or both. But until recently, we could patronize restaurants on whatever basis we chose, including whether or not they allow smoking. Then liberals decided that personal choice wasn't good enough anymore. In many states, they moved to outlaw smoking in restaurants "for the good of everyone."

The conservative leaves these choices up to the people. We say you're responsible enough to choose a restaurant that either bans or allows smoking. Nobody should tell restaurant owners how to run their own businesses—nobody should impose their definition of "what's best" on everybody else. But liberals decided that since *they* don't like smoking in restaurants, then *nobody* should be allowed to smoke in restaurants, regardless of what the owners or the customers want. They said it's a matter of your health, and then they decided that your health was their business.

Eating right, exercising, and lifting boxes with your legs instead of your back are also matters of health. Should we pass laws to mandate these things, too? Where will it end?

Here's a hint: on the campaign trail, then-Senator Obama declared, "[W]e can't drive our SUVs and eat as much as we want and keep our homes on 72 degrees at all times . . . and then just expect that other countries are going to say OK. . . . That's not leadership. That's not going to happen." So I hope you weren't expecting that under this administration you'd be able to drive whatever car you want, eat whatever food you want, or heat your house to whatever temperature you want. Obama was clear as a bell: "That's not going to happen."

Liberals' increasing intolerance reflects a disturbing hubris in the liberal mindset. When someone is so sure they are right about morality, ethics, science, economics, and anything else that they foreclose on the choices of others, we have entered dangerous territory for individual rights. Liberals often justify their coercive schemes by claiming they are acting "for the public good," to save lives, to save the country, or even to save the earth. For liberals, spinning arrogance as altruism is an art form.

The denial of personal choice violates basic American ideals of life, liberty, and the pursuit of happiness, and also does long-term damage to the nation. Just look at how the Obama administration has tried to ram through Congress the cap-and-trade bill, healthcare reform, and other transformative policies that would immensely expand government and curtail our freedom: they've pushed them with almost no bipartisan support, often without providing enough time to fully debate the massive bills or even to read them. By rejecting the "post-partisan" consensus we were promised during President Obama's campaign, liberals reduce the need for us to listen to each other, reason carefully, and respect the opinions of others. *Why bother explaining why you're right if you can just make people do what you think they ought to?* This is the point at which leaders stop acting like fellow citizens and start acting like domineering, out-of-touch autocrats. Taking away individual choice robs people of a measure of their dignity, no matter the "social benefit" liberals insist will come as repayment.

REPUBLICANS REJECT IDENTITY POLITICS.

Considering people primarily as members of racial, ethnic, or gender-based groups or of social classes instead of individuals is called "identity politics." Those who subscribe to it believe the benefits of society should accrue to groups that can demonstrate the greatest victimhood and that those blamed for this oppression should be punished.

A lot of bad ideas flow from categorizing people as either victims or oppressors: the redistribution of wealth, punitive taxation, hostility toward traditional values, and the abandonment of individual rights, to name a few. But liberals are enthralled by identity politics, largely because it requires big government to shift resources from society's "oppressors" to its "victims."

Liberals typically sell their policies by reducing policy debates to issues of identity politics or of class struggle. It is so much easier—and therefore, so tempting—to think of "all women," "all African-Americans," "all gay people," or "all poor people" as uniform groups whose members think exactly the same about every issue, instead of considering what any individual man or woman might want or need or believe.

By elevating groups over individuals, liberals become obligated to stifle different ideas. Why? Because liberals need to enforce a groupthink mentality so that no one questions the assumptions liberals make about each identity group. If those assumptions are undermined, the justification for liberal policies based on those assumptions is also undermined. Thus, liberals not only end up stigmatizing original thinking, they also refuse to consider individuals "by the content of their character," as Martin Luther King Jr. proclaimed we should. Instead, and in great and sad irony, identity politics has led liberals to circle back in defense of what they claim to hate: judging people by the color of their skin.

This helps explain why liberals vilify African-American conservatives. Their very existence undermines the stereotypes liberals have created to legitimize their power structure. And many minorities, particularly black people, would likely reject that power structure if they realized that the Democratic Party views them largely as a simple stereotype—poor, paralyzed people, with no control over their own destiny, entirely dependent on government benevolence. The entire worldview of Democrats today is really a profound negation of the ideal of equality that propelled the American civil rights movement. This kind of prejudiced thinking is the logical endpoint when you begin with the liberal assumption that human beings are a mere representation of some predetermined characteristics. People come to matter less as individuals and more as interchangeable parts of some grand race- or gender- or class-based scheme.

Principle begets policy, and policy defines action. Thus, liberals engage in ever-expanding and never-ending preference politics rather than basing policy on a fair examination of what you can do as an individual. The quintessential example of this is found in Democratic judicial appointments, especially to the Supreme Court. For his first nominee, President Obama chose someone who personifies identity politics, Sonia Sotomayor, who famously stated her belief that a "wise Latina" judge would typically make better rulings than a white male. Sotomayor has also asserted that "our gender and national origins may and will make a difference in our judging." This appalling obsession with racial difference, with comparing the innate abilities of different racial groups, and with writing these differences into judicial rulings and public policy, is at the core of the liberal agenda today.

Identity politics is political warfare, pure and simple, and liberals use it to divide people by class, ethnicity, gender, or whatever is most useful at the moment. In pursuit of their own vision of a better society, they pit one group of people against another by fomenting jealousy and distrust, whipping folks into a frenzy for the sake of acquiring ever-more control over our lives.

The angrier and more distrustful we are of one another, the more people become convinced that their individualism is not nearly as valuable as their group identity—if the nation is composed of nothing more than competing groups, the only safe place to be is in one of those groups. And since liberals promise to protect this or that group at the expense of others, citizenship becomes a constant struggle to stay in the good graces of those in charge. Whoever belongs to the most sympathetic group with the most empathetic friends in power gets rewarded with the most benefits from government.

Thus the individual counts not for who he is, but for who his friends are, what he looks like, and how much of a victim he can make of himself. That is liberalism. And that's no way to run a country.

JUDICIAL ACTIVISM SUBVERTS THE CONSTITUTION.

The great challenge of modern governance is finding a fair and just principle to resolve the natural conflicts between the interests of individuals and the state. To strike the right balance between these interests, conservatives look to American history. Our country was founded, explored, and expanded by rugged individualists—people who jealously guarded their freedom and who met their obligation to community most often through the moral requirements of their religion or personal moral code.

This system was codified in our Constitution. It isn't a perfect system, but it works pretty damn well. It has been the foundation for the most powerful economy on earth and it has brought the highest standard of living to the most people throughout history, while being flexible enough to accommodate new freedoms as times have changed. The self-responsibility and self-control at the heart of that culture is what we speak of today when we talk about "a Christian nation"—not that everyone is a Christian, but that American morality reflects the values of the largely Christian population that built up the nation in its first two centuries.

Liberals, on the other hand, believe in a much stronger government role, to the detriment of individual freedom. Since this vision contradicts America's historic values and the spirit of the Constitution, it has rarely found much support in state legislatures or in Congress. Frustrated with slow progress on their agenda, liberals discovered they could bypass the will of the people by appealing to like-minded judges to diminish individual freedom by judicial fiat. This is the essence of the modern argument over "judicial restraint." In short, liberals believe that many matters are too important to be trusted to the people and their elected representatives to decide. Instead, they seek to reinterpret the law—and often to make law from the bench—without having to persuade the voters.

The drafting of the Constitution was a historic achievement. No document since the Magna Carta had so carefully and clearly defined how a people should govern themselves. Indeed, the Constitution's words must be interpreted according to their literal meaning, not according to the mood of the times or the personal opinions of a judge. That is what was intended by the Founders, who foresaw a nation of laws, not of men. In both a practical and a philosophical sense, this separates justice from passion.

The Founders created a system of checks and balances to diminish the opportunity for abuse in our governing system. But someone can always find a way around the rules, at least for a little while. Many liberals now see their ideas as so unquestionable, and their opponents' ideas as so misguided, that they no longer even care how they get their ideas into law, as long as it happens. Thus, liberals have embraced judicial activism, relying on unelected judges to usurp the role of Congress and legislate from the bench.

With liberal control of the White House, the House of Representatives, and the Senate, the opportunity for abusing federal power is magnified. Jay Nordlinger, a writer for *National Review*, summed up the potential for damage this way:

> Governmental power is an awesome, sometimes terrifying thing. It can be a terrible bully. And those who hold power should be mindful of that. They should have a deep sense of humility about the power that has been placed in their care.... I simply fear that, for much of the Democratic party—and some of the Republican party—government power is a club with which to beat those you dislike, merrily.

When we forget that government power comes from the people, we open the door to a coercive government that no longer protects the rights of all of us. Government becomes increasingly concerned with protecting those in power—that is, those who make the rules. Republicans do not—and will not—try to one-up the Democrats by getting our own policies legislated from the bench. We will continue to appoint judges who adhere strictly to the Constitution and to the law as written. To pass laws, we rely on the democratic process, depending solely on our elected representatives, not activist judges.

One of the most obvious issues affected by activist judges is the constant attempt by liberals to whittle away the Second Amendment. If liberals want to cut off Americans' right to keep and bear arms, there is a way to do so—persuade Americans to vote to repeal the Second Amendment. But liberals won't try that, because they know the American people would never agree. Instead, they spend millions of dollars and thousands of hours filing lawsuits in search of liberal judges who are willing to rule that the law and the Constitution mean something besides what the words say. It's the only way liberals can impose their extreme anti-individualist ideas on the rest of us.

Ironically, one of the greatest supporters of a careful and restrained reading of law and the Constitution was also one of the most influential liberals of the twentieth century. Nominated to the Supreme Court by FDR, Felix Frankfurter helped found the American Civil Liberties Union and was one of the architects of the New Deal. But unlike many modern liberals, Justice Frankfurter believed that the creation of policy is the responsibility of legislators and that judges have no business crafting laws from the bench. He understood that judges have a narrow, specific job: to interpret the law only to the extent necessary in any given case. He knew that his personal beliefs should have no impact on how he decided a case; he knew that the question was always, "What did the elected officials write in the applicable law, and what does the Constitution say?" For him, the question was never, "Whose circumstance does Justice Frankfurter find most empathetic?"

In his famous dissent in *West Virginia Board of Education v. Barnette* (1943), Justice Frankfurter put it succinctly:

[A]s judges we are neither Jew, nor Gentile, neither Catholic, nor agnostic. We owe equal attach-
ment to the Constitution and are equally bound by
our judicial obligations, whether we derive our citizenship from the earliest or the latest immigrants
to these shores. As a member of this Court I am
not justified in writing my private notions of policy
into the Constitution, no matter how deeply I may
cherish them or how mischievous I may deem
their disregard.

How I wish we had more liberals like him today.

LIMITED GOVERNMENT IS THE KEY TO RESTRAINING THE TEMPTATIONS OF POWER.

By presenting their ideas as essential "for the public good," liberals replace individual choice with federal or state edict. Naturally,
this leads to more and more power for the government. After all,
more regulation of your behavior requires more government to
administer and enforce those regulations. If the law didn't for-
malize and demand so many obligations, we wouldn't need a big
government—we would take care of most things on our own.

Government is a coercive power; that is, you have to do what
government requires or it can punish you in the form of a fine,
jail time, or restrictions on your business or behavior. And liberals believe that a steady expansion of this coercive power is necessary to guarantee "fair" and "just" social outcomes.

But power is tempting, and humans are not very good at resisting temptation. This is where liberalism shifts from being a bad idea to a profoundly corrupting one: with so much power concentrated in one place, liberals cannot resist using that power not only to "improve" society, but to "improve" people as well.

These days, liberals attempt (and often succeed) in using government to force you to eat the "right" food, drive the "right" car, send your children to the "right" school, and believe in the "right" ideology. Liberals actively and aggressively use your government and your tax dollars to promote ideas and activities that they believe every "enlightened" individual ought to support—and they're not shy about using your children's school curricula in this task. Today, liberals in the federal government spend your money less on building up a society that rewards hard work and fair play, and more on advancing their partisan agenda of socialized healthcare, global warming alarmism, and redistributing wealth. And it's time for Republicans to expose this abuse of power, strip away that power, and give it back to the people.

Some liberals respond this way: "We won the election, so we get to do what we want." This is like a football team winning a coin toss, then declaring it gets to set the rules of the game. In a January 2009 meeting, a Republican senator challenged Obama on the extravagant size of his "stimulus" spending plan. Obama replied with two words: "I won."

But winning an election, like winning a coin toss, is just the beginning of the game. It gives you the privilege of making a few key choices about the direction things should go. It doesn't mean you can change the rules. It *does* mean that now you get to do the hard part—play the game within the rules. Yet here is what liberals do: they take the coercive power of government and use it to change the rules and choose the winners and losers. And of course, a lot of people are willing to spend a great deal of money to make sure the administration chooses them as a winner. The *Washington Times* reported in October 2009 that the Obama administration is rewarding big Democratic donors with ambassadorships, special briefings, VIP access to the White House, and other perks. So if Bill Clinton turned the White House into a hotel and coffee shop, President Obama has now turned it into a full service resort complete with amenities for the highest Democrat bidder.

The responsible position, of course, is to follow the Constitutional mandate of equal rights for all. But to paraphrase George Orwell, liberals believe that some people are "more equal" than others.

Government has a coercive power that other institutions do not. We can choose to change churches, quit a club, or refuse to shop at places we don't like. But when it comes to government, we have no choice but to submit. Conservatives see all this as a reason to limit government. Liberals see this as an excellent reason to expand it.

And that's the core difference between liberal principles and our own.

STEP

7

Contrast Our Principles with Theirs, Part II

Tolerance, Equal Rights, and a Culture of Freedom

IN 2002, Congressman Bob Ehrlich approached me to be his running mate in his campaign to become governor of Maryland. It was an uphill battle—no Republican had won the office since Spiro Agnew squeaked out a victory in 1966. We would be competing against then-rising Democratic star Kathleen Kennedy Townsend, the daughter of Robert F. Kennedy and niece of Ted Kennedy.

Running an unconventional campaign, we wooed a significant number of Democrats to our side—a necessity in a heavily

Democrat state. We built coalitions and met with diverse civic, religious, and political groups in their neighborhoods and places of worship. Ultimately, we made history as the first winning Republican ticket for the Maryland governorship in forty years. We beat back the status quo when many said it simply could not be done.

So I know a little something about winning against the odds—something Republicans can do across the entire nation at this crucial time in our country's history. America needs Republican ideas now more than ever. It's time for the GOP to rise to the occasion, it's time to make our voices heard, and it's time to serve our country and our fellow citizens.

The Democrats want us to be silent. You've heard their self-serving claim that if we oppose President Obama's policies we are somehow rooting against American success—though they didn't hesitate to oppose President Bush's policies, did they? But their bullying won't stop us from speaking the truth. We would be abandoning our responsibility if we were to be silent while they spend our country into the abyss, while they borrow money America doesn't have and that our children and grandchildren will somehow have to repay, and while they usher in the most massive expansion of federal control in the history of our republic.

Now is the time for Republicans to clearly define our outlook, one that stands in marked contrast to the Democrats' insistence on the increasingly heavy hand of government. We must explain our principles clearly and forcefully, directing our appeal to the American people as a whole—not to balkanized racial groups and competing special interests. Most important, we should constantly demonstrate what all people stand to gain from policies that promote freedom, personal responsibility, educational choice, and strong families.

TOLERANCE IS REQUIRED. APPROVAL IS NOT.

A lot of things puzzle me about liberals, but few things puzzle me more than their say-one-thing-but-do-the-opposite attitude toward tolerance. For people who spend so much time and energy claiming to "empower" people, they sure have a lot of problems with people empowering themselves.

When it comes to conservatism and Republicans, many otherwise reasonable and normal people of the liberal persuasion throw basic civility out the window. They embrace a frighteningly intense opposition to—and in many cases, open hatred of—conservatives, conservatism, and Republicans.

Vicious political exchanges are nothing new. Read the political discourse going back to America's founding and you'll find very little that hasn't been duplicated across many angry Left websites and blogs. But what's scary about modern political discourse is the open desire of many on the Left to shut down the voice of the opposition—to narrow by statute the limits of "acceptable" opinion and to stigmatize certain opinions, especially traditional ideas about marriage and the family. The Left increasingly seeks to isolate people with whom they disagree and banish their proposals from the marketplace of ideas. For example, I recently learned from former President Jimmy Carter that I, along with tens of millions of Americans, am racist because I oppose President Obama's agenda. That was a real revelation.

Think back. Republicans were vehemently opposed to President Clinton on matters of character and policy, but I don't know a single Republican who tried to silence any of Clinton's supporters or those who implemented his policies.

By contrast, witness nearly a decade of what is now called "Bush Derangement Syndrome": the kneejerk opposition to every position taken by President George W. Bush. Now that they have governing majorities, many liberals are trying retroactively to *criminalize* President Bush's policies. Liberals overwhelmingly opposed Bush's national security policies, and that is their right. But when they appoint a special prosecutor to investigate CIA interrogators—patriotic Americans who undertook a difficult and sometimes dangerous job geared toward preventing terrorist attacks—they are undermining a key national security agency in order to banish certain policies from public consideration.

The same intent is evident at the University of California at Berkley, where protestors have repeatedly staged demonstrations demanding the firing and prosecution of Law Professor John Yoo, who advised the Bush Administration on terrorist detainee policies. The goal of all this is not just to denounce Yoo, the CIA interrogators, or any other individual; it's to intimidate anyone who might publicly support the "wrong" policies in the future. "Cross us," the protestors are saying, "and this is what's in store for you. You'll never live quietly again." I shudder at the thought that Americans of any political persuasion could be so consumed with hate of their fellow American that they'd be willing to destroy their perceived opponents' lives and undermine the nation's security in order to achieve a political "victory."

Liberals say they believe in free speech, but then cheer when one of their own shouts down or hurls a pie at a conservative speaker, or pressures a university into canceling a speech by a conservative. When concerned citizens show up to townhall meetings to grill their representatives about the Democrats' healthcare plans, however, they're denounced by liberals as a fascist mob. Likewise, liberals hector us about the need to "tolerate" every lifestyle choice and belief system, no matter how exotic—except Christianity, which they relentlessly denigrate.

Liberals now recognize all sorts of vague exceptions to freedom of speech, such as "hate speech." Words can be tremendously hurtful, but generation after generation of Americans has wisely accepted this as the price we pay for broad freedom of expression. Even many liberals once agreed that one person's "hate speech" is another person's free expression.

But few liberals agree anymore, leading to ever-more outrageous calls for suppression and censorship. Speaker of the House Nancy Pelosi recently gained a lot of attention with her ominous warning that critics of President Obama's healthcare reform risk fomenting violence by mentally unstable people. She spoke about the need "to carefully balance" freedom and safety, for she heard "this kind of rhetoric" in San Francisco in the 1970s, when it "created a climate in which violence took place." She added, "Our country is great because people can say what they think and they believe, but I also think that they have to take responsibility for any incitement that they may cause."

Speaker Pelosi's statement implies an important question: if this rhetoric really creates a climate that leads to violence, then should this rhetoric be allowed at all? She elected not to address the question directly, but her comments certainly laid the groundwork for charging the Democrats' critics with incitement to violence. Look at the elements of her remarks: talking vaguely about the need to balance freedom and safety; references to possible violence by unnamed, unhinged people; labeling criticism as "incitement"; and of course, ritual praise for freedom of speech followed by the word "but."

This has also becoming a disturbingly common aspect of the Left's crusade against global warming: similar to Paul Krugman's hysterical pronouncements, in 2008, NASA climate scientist James Hansen told Congress that energy company CEOs who doubt global warming should be "tried for high crimes against humanity and nature." Likewise, at the Live Earth concert in 2007, Robert F. Kennedy Jr. told a cheering crowd that such skeptics are committing "treason." He added, "And we need to start treating them as traitors."

Tolerance for ideas is a foundation of self-government and civil society, and Democrats are undermining it every day. They used to stand up for all opinions, especially unpopular ones. They prided themselves on it. It's a hard position to maintain, though, and they've long since given it up.

If the Obama administration really values open debate, then why has it declared virtually all-out war on Fox News? In October 2009, White House aides launched a concerted campaign against Fox, arguing that it should not be considered a legitimate news network and that other news outlets should ignore its stories. Obama's lieutenants have heaped similar vituperation on Rush Limbaugh, the insurance industry, the Chamber of Commerce, and just about anyone else who has criticized any of their Dear Leader's "transformative" proposals.

It's shocking how little tolerance this administration has for dissent—an act that the Left upheld as the pinnacle of patriotism during the Bush presidency. But what can you really expect when the White House communications effort was led by a woman, Anita Dunn, who cites Communist mass-murderer Mao Tse-tung as one of her favorite "political philosophers"?

Lately the Left has tried to gut the First Amendment by shutting down conservative talk radio. Their excuse? The results of the free market, in which conservative talk radio has thrived and liberal talk radio has foundered, are "unfair." (Strangely, they don't argue much about the fairness of the Obama lovefest on CNN, MSNBC, CBS, ABC, NBC, and government-sponsored NPR and PBS.)

And keep in mind, there's a bastion of liberalism that's even less open to dissent than either the radical environmental movement or the Democratic Party. If you want a *real* dose of liberal intolerance, try visiting one of our nation's universities, saying something the least bit conservative, and, well . . . let me know how that works out for you.

An awful lot of liberals don't understand what most conservatives know by heart: that tolerance only really matters when you're tolerating opinions and ideas that aren't your own. If you can't show tolerance toward those with whom you disagree, you're practicing the worst kind of intolerance.

Regardless of party, we are, as Americans, obliged to be tolerant because it is elemental to the "live and let live" philosophy that defines liberty, and it is the basis for a healthy marketplace of ideas. Liberals should remember that true diversity is not limited to skin color and sexual orientation. True diversity is true tolerance of free expression—even expressions that offend liberal ideals.

Now, tolerance and approval are different things, mind you. We're not required to like one another based on what religion we practice, our sexual orientation, our political beliefs, or the color of our skin. You may want the approval of your fellow Americans for how you live, but the fact is that you can't require it of them— not personally, and not by law. The only thing we can require of each other is to respect the fact that every citizen is entitled to his or her own beliefs and has the right to express them. This used to unite Democrats and Republicans. Maybe it will again, someday. But tolerance goes hand in hand with personal freedom and individual rights—values that liberals are increasingly abandoning in favor of big government. So for now, Republicans stand alone as representatives of true tolerance.

The right to assemble, to speak freely, and to believe as one wishes are not just words on paper that we promote when it's easy or convenient or advantageous for our side. They were established at our nation's founding so we could govern ourselves civilly; by consensus on matters of debate and by principle on matters of greater truth. They weren't pronounced so one side or the other could make a claim on having all the answers, and they didn't include exceptions for the opponents of whomever happens to be in power.

REPUBLICANS BELIEVE IN EQUAL RIGHTS WITHOUT REGARD TO RACE.

Some people accuse our party of being disinterested in civil rights and in the black community. They're wrong. The Republican

Party, in fact, has an inextricable link to African-Americans forged in the bonds of history.

For over one hundred years, Republicans led the effort to guarantee the basic human rights of black citizens. It began when President Abraham Lincoln fought the secession of the South over slavery, and continued with Lincoln's signing of the Emancipation Proclamation in 1863. After the Civil War ended, so-called "Radical Republicans" stood up to Democrats to pass the first Civil Rights Act in 1866, which legally recognized blacks as U.S. citizens.

Despite losing some black support during FDR's presidency, the Republicans remained strongly committed to equality throughout the twentieth century—it was overwhelming Republican support that guaranteed passage of the Civil Rights Act of 1964. But increasing political and economic tensions within the African-American community, coupled with the Republican Party's lukewarm attitude toward the civil rights movement, led many African-Americans to believe that the Party of Lincoln had left them behind. And so they chose another party.

Today, the Republican Party and the post-civil-rights generations of African-Americans face an intriguing challenge that can be summarized by a Chinese proverb: "The best time to plant a tree was twenty years ago. The second best time is today." The challenge for Republicans is to recognize that now is the time to plant the tree of hope and opportunity for this and future generations of African-Americans.

For African-Americans, we must recognize that the battle for civil rights in the twentieth century has become a struggle for economic prosperity in the twenty-first. Generations before us fought for the right to sit at the lunch counter, but it should be this generation's goal to own the diner! African-Americans came to this country as slaves but through our indomitable spirit, we have emerged as architects of our own future, with a vital stake in the future of America as well.

Founded on the fundamental principle that all Americans should be guaranteed human and civil rights, the Republican Party should once again become the natural home of the black community. But we shouldn't try to beat the Democrats in the racial spoils game. Instead, we must reach out to African-Americans with the same approach we should take toward all Americans: by stressing our unyielding commitment to legal equality and individual rights.

We Republicans recognize that though we may come from different backgrounds and cultures, the strength of our nation lies with the individual and his or her own dignity, freedom, and initiative to succeed. These qualities are not something government created or gave to us. They are ours by birth, and they must be cultivated and maintained by the people. These qualities define us as American.

REPUBLICANS PROMOTE INDEPENDENCE AND FREEDOM, NOT GOVERNMENT DEPENDENCE.

Many years after my father died from alcoholism, I spoke with my mother about that time in her life. How did she feel? What did she think? What was her struggle? And she talked about the great weight of not knowing—not knowing how to pay the bills, not knowing where to turn for a friendly ear, not knowing how best to educate her children for the world ahead. In short, she wondered how to do more than survive from one day to the next without her husband. She recounted to me that many friends and family members encouraged or even insisted that she accept public assistance.

"Get the check," she remembered them saying.

I asked her why she hadn't done that and her response was pure Maebell: "I didn't want the government to raise my kids."

Maebell didn't think somebody from the government was going to show up at her door and make her tell my sister and me to do our homework and pick up our rooms. But she understood that when you accept help from government, you are entering into a bargain. If government can give you what you need to live, it can also take it away. And the more you depend on government, the more invested you are in keeping government big and powerful—for your own sake—even if that costs you some freedom. After all, you've got to feed your family.

So my mother never "got the check," never signed up for help from the government, never asked for a thing. She just wanted to raise her family on her own terms as an example for her children.

It's in the liberals' political interest to create dependency, because it creates a need for more and more government. This works on multiple levels. When government gives out "good things," those who receive the benefits and don't have to pay for them are happy to give their votes to anyone who promises to keep the spigot open. But there's an even more powerful way for liberals to get votes. Just think how much more certain those votes will be when a citizen relies on government not for a benefit here or there, but for the basic elements of life. When you consider that context, government-run healthcare seems less urgent for the people, and more urgent for the fortunes of the Democratic Party.

CULTURE SHOULD BE CREATED BY OUR INDIVIDUAL CHOICES AND VALUES, NOT BY GOVERNMENT AND LIBERAL ELITES.

One of the most difficult challenges we all face is deciding how much influence government should have in shaping our culture. There is no clear-cut answer and no simple test, because the problem is a matter of opinion, faith, and conviction. We disagree, often profoundly, over which virtues and values to elevate, which to mute, and what the role of government ought to be in doing so.

But one thing is for sure: government *will* have a strong influence on culture. We can try to keep government out of it, but the very act of governing encourages some behaviors and discourages others. There is no abdicating from those choices; to govern is to choose, sometimes directly and sometimes indirectly.

The government's influence on culture is marked by two poles. On one end, pure libertarianism calls for the complete disengagement of government from individual life. That sounds like total freedom, but the lack of any rules yields anarchy. On the other end of the spectrum, pure liberalism, at least as it's practiced today, calls for vigorous government intervention in nearly every aspect of life—in family, healthcare, commerce, speech, and more. Because liberals value people less as individuals than as members of victimized groups, they believe that empowered "experts" (or "czars," or whatever else they call these supposedly enlightened bureaucrats) will create a "fairer" world for those groups. But this denial and destruction of so much human choice ultimately leads to little more than smiley-faced totalitarianism.

Conservatives believe culture should raise up the fundamental qualities of civilization: liberty and respect for human life. Beyond that, we believe a nation's culture reflects the character of its citizens. We express our character through our individual actions, and so we create culture simply by living according to our principles. This is the most democratic (small-d) approach to culture—especially compared to the liberals' approach, which is to use culture as just another tool for controlling your behavior.

Once again, conservative principles trump liberal principles on both moral and practical grounds. Conservatives' primary concern is individual rights, and we are naturally suspicious of the concentration of power in a few hands. We say, "Trust individual liberty to produce the greatest culture." Liberals say, "Trust me—government—to create culture, because I know what culture is best for you."

Now, don't get me wrong. I don't have it in for government. I just like my government in small—very small—portions.

Government as our forefathers planned it has a purpose, and that purpose is limited and narrow. It is to help maintain a society in which people are free to live their lives as they see fit. That means as *they* see fit, not according to what government leaders decide to let you do.

Government, while vital to our ability to live together in a civilized way, should never be extended beyond its Constitutional limits; to do so makes government a big pain in the behind. Government becomes an even bigger burden when it is allowed to dictate outcomes, choose winners and losers, and determine what is best for you, your family, your community, and your business.

There is a perception among some people that the Republican Party is more interested in governing private life than in governing the nation. People got that idea because, sometimes, we really do seem that way. But it's not true. On any given day, we just want government to get out of the way and let us do what the Founders intended.

Our principles are right, but we have not always talked about them effectively. We need to communicate our values, not impose them. And the perpetual media attack on Republicans yields a distorted public image of what we believe. Our heart is not in telling you how to live your life. Our heart is in helping you appreciate the value of life and the potential of living free. The Founders did not write about "life, liberty, and the pursuit of happiness" because they liked the sound of the words. They intended for Americans to be able to pursue the things that were inalienable to them. Our job is to replace the media-distorted version of our rights and beliefs with what the Founders intended.

The challenge can be summed up in a remark I heard recently from a young man in his mid-twenties. He said, "It's enough for me to try to live how my pastor tells me to live on

Sunday. I don't need a political party telling me how to live my life Monday through Saturday."

Just so.

WHAT'S PAST IS PAST.

Guess what? Nobody can change the past. So why do we waste so much time in politics talking about it and trying to rewrite it? It's time for liberals to stop whining about how Republicans ran the federal government under President Bush. They're in charge now, and it's time they took responsibility for the consequences of their own actions and policies.

Republicans also need to look forward and not behind, because the world is entering into a very uncertain era. There is no room—and there should be no tolerance—for indecision, excuses, missed opportunities, and poor choices. Let's acknowledge what gets done right, learn from what goes wrong, and press on.

The path ahead is always uncharted territory, and every decision will have some uncertainty to it. So while our policies must be informed by the past, we should not give in to the occasional temptation to romanticize "the good old days." We must constantly re-evaluate our policies to ensure they are the optimal prescription for any given time, and that once implemented, they work as intended. Let's rely on character, principle, and a forward-looking mindset as the hallmarks of our party. If the Democrats insist on becoming a fossilized party dedicated to re-fighting past battles, we won't need to set them straight—the voters will do it for us.

Contrast Our Principles with Theirs, Part III

Economics, the Justice System, and National Security

THERE IS a famous saying attributed to the Chinese: "May you live in interesting times."

That describes today pretty well, don't you think?

We Republicans now face choices that are not only "interesting"—in both good and bad ways—but also vital. We must define the very nature of conservatism in the post-Reagan era, a time that renders commonsense conservatism not just an improvement, but a radical improvement over the status quo.

The times have changed. Many personal priorities and attitudes are significantly different than they were just a decade ago.
Demographics are in upheaval. Ever-improving technology has
rewired vast swaths of culture and commerce. The world in general and Americans in particular hunger for new ideas. President
Obama was elected by promising something new, but that turned
out to be a retread of big-government liberalism salvaged from
the scrapheap of history and deserving to go back there. Obama's
sinking popularity indicates Americans are already starting to
realize they were sold a false bill of goods. There's nothing more
sobering to voters than buyers' remorse.

So Americans are still searching for new ideas, and this represents an opportunity for conservatives to present fresh proposals and win the confidence of a new generation of voters.
Republican leaders must demonstrate they are prepared to lead
in changing times with vision, strength, and humility. We must
offer practical policies that help solve problems people face today.

There is no magic formula and no secret potion that will
gain new adherents to our cause. Ideological buzzwords and
partisan cheerleading has never been enough, and it sure won't
be adequate today. We have to identify the problems that government is ill-equipped to address and come up with ways to
make a real difference. That means finding answers for the family struggling to live paycheck to paycheck; answers for rolling
back the reach of an increasingly intrusive government; answers
for reversing the erosion of our Constitutional rights; answers
to turn around the liberal co-opting of American education; and
answers to protect families against the liberal onslaught to
diminish their importance.

We should craft new policies to meet these needs, without regard for ingratiating ourselves with the liberal media or the Democrats. Our agenda should be based on core conservative principles:

- Conservatives believe in the power and ingenuity of individuals to create the legacy of a nation through hard work, self-discipline, and respect for each other.
- Conservatives believe government should be limited so that it never becomes powerful enough to take away the rights of the individual.
- Conservatives believe in low taxes so that individuals can keep more of their own money and empower themselves economically.
- Conservatives believe in limited regulation of business so that we encourage entrepreneurs to take reasonable risks, thus allowing more individuals to achieve the fruits of self-made success.
- Conservatives believe in the ideal of a colorblind society so that each man and woman is considered first to be an individual and not simply a member of some hyphenated class or group.

Democrats are less interested in people as individuals and more interested in people as members of oppressed groups. They are less interested in making life better for American citizens than in making government loom larger in our lives. But Republicans must always remember that unlike the "change" President Obama promised in 2008, we have the opportunity to bring change through policies that actually help people and that reinforce the basic beliefs and values of the American people.

THERE CANNOT BE TRUE LIBERTY WITHOUT ECONOMIC LIBERTY.

A person is not truly free unless that freedom includes economic liberty: the right to private property; the right to make, buy and sell what he pleases, as he pleases; and the right to keep what he earns. This sounds so obvious to most folks that their first reaction is to wonder how such rights could be denied to anyone in America. Yet liberals do it all the time.

The diminshing of economic liberty is one of the primary goals of modern liberalism. Of course, they don't call it that. When they cut back or eliminate parts of your financial freedom, they do it under the guise of protecting one person or group from the predations of someone else. As a consequence, and given President Obama's rush to socialize the nation's economy and his desire to be the Dr. Phil of race relations, it is increasingly clear that such core beliefs are lost on Democrats.

In the economic realm, this takes the form of egregious regulations on products that drive up prices, drive down consumer choice, and strangle creativity and productivity. Let's get it out in the open: liberals just don't trust the free market. But Republicans believe that you have the right to make your own economic choices for you and your family, which has been engraved in the American psyche since the Revolution.

Liberals no longer remember or no longer care that America was largely established out of a crisis of economic liberty. When men such as Reverend Jonathan Mayhew and the lawyer James Otis Jr. denounced "taxation without representation" as tyranny, they were speaking against the power of England to tax citizens who had no say in whether they were taxed, or how they were taxed, or for what purposes their taxes would be spent. It was the first act in a long American tradition of fighting back against those in government who try to take away what is rightfully ours. A limit on your ability to buy and sell and spend and trade is a limit on everything else you do.

When government controls your wallet, bank account, or means to earn a living, then it controls the basic elements of your life.

THE FIRST CONCERN OF OUR SYSTEM OF JUSTICE SHOULD BE JUSTICE ITSELF.

When I was a boy, I always knew that if I bucked the rules there would be consequences. Maebell had a distinct way of reminding me of that. Whether it was abiding by the curfew, performing my chores, always telling the truth even when it was hard, or keeping the other rules in our home, I knew that breaking the rules meant swift and certain punishment.

In our homes and in our personal lives, rules matter. In society, the rule of law matters. Many Americans are rightly frustrated that when some people break the rules, other people fall all over themselves to excuse the offense and prevent any punishment.

One of the main purposes of our justice system is to impose punishments in order to discourage lawbreaking—but that doesn't get talked about much anymore. Just as liberals have expanded the pedagogical mission of schools to the point that basic education in math, science, history, and English is shockingly diluted, they have also stretched and distorted the role of our system of justice.

Our justice system is designed to enforce the rules of an ordered society. For society to have confidence in that system, we have to know that anti-social actions, such as the commission of a crime, will lead to negative consequences. Yet most of us realize that an army of lawmakers, lawyers, judges, and reporters now sees crime not as a threat to society, but as the fault of society. Hence we now live in the "Age of the Victim," in which those who suffer at the hands of criminals are blamed for the criminals' behavior. Never mind the circumstances of the real victim or the family or even the community affected by criminal acts.

And the Left is quick to chastise us with a long, sympathetic description of the life circumstances of convicted criminals, but they rarely detail for us what criminals really do to their victims, or the devastating effect on families that lose someone to crime. And you never hear a word about how the lack of swift and certain punishment makes us all more likely to be victims of crime.

The system should incorporate drug counseling, education efforts, and other programs to treat and rehabilitate prisoners, depending on each program's record of effectiveness. But these cannot replace the swift and certain punishment of criminals, which is the essential element of the entire justice system. Justice is the framework of an ordered society. When the purpose of justice is obscured by sympathy-mongering for criminals, the result is the dissolution of order in society. And that affects all of us.

AMERICA IS THE GREATEST BEACON FOR FREEDOM AND OPPORTUNITY THAT THE WORLD WILL EVER KNOW.

From an idea was born a nation that would speak to the best instincts of men and women around the world. It would affirm for them that all things are possible. It would be that singular flame guiding its people along a pathway to the one thing that matters most: freedom.

From an idea was born the proper relationship between man and government. It would be the foundation for the liberating truth that man has an unalienable right to govern himself.

From an idea was born the link between a new nation and freedom, prosperity, and opportunity.

From an idea was born a peerless and profound appreciation for life, liberty, and the pursuit of happiness.

From an idea was born a place called America.

As Republicans, our policies should demonstrate the wisdom of the American experiment and our commitment to freedom. America has made mistakes, and we will make mistakes in the future—that's just common sense. But the American ideal of liberty and justice for all is no mistake. It is a beacon of hope for people everywhere. It's become fashionable in the current administration to apologize for America and blame her for the world's problems, but Republicans know the real source of the world's problems is the absence of liberty. Liberals may not appreciate the vitality of the American ideal, but Republicans do, and so do the masses of people who immigrate here, and the millions more who dream of doing so. That fact should come through in every policy we propose.

Here's some unsolicited advice for Barack Obama: the president of the freest nation on earth won't bring people to liberty by traveling around the world making apologies on behalf of her citizens and making nice with fascists and tyrants. Bad guys are bad guys, and if they don't like us, I'd say that's a pretty good sign we're doing things right.

We don't have to prove over and over why America is the greatest nation in the history of civilization. Don't believe me? Look at the line of people waiting to get in, and all those breaking the law to get here. Liberals may not like the America of today, and they may believe that the rest of the world feels the same way, but a whole lot of the world is putting the lie to their claim—and they're doing it by getting here any way they can.

Come to think of it, I don't see many, if any, liberals headed for the exits either.

TALKING WON'T ALWAYS BE ENOUGH TO STOP EVIL PEOPLE AND REGIMES FROM HURTING OR KILLING US.

You can't reason with everybody.

The world is a dangerous place, and there are some dangerous individuals and regimes that won't go away simply through appeasement or accommodation or because President Obama imagines that everybody loves him. History is filled with tragic examples. There are people in the world who hate Jews, and no amount of discussion and no pile of concessions is going to change their minds. If the Holocaust didn't get them to appreciate "never again," how in the world is a sweet-sounding speech going to do it? It's not a matter of reason to them, it's an inarguable conviction that runs through some souls and some cultures. There are people in the world who hate black people too, and no roundtable discussion or heart-to-heart talk is going to enlighten them. And there are people and regimes in the world who hate America not for what we have or have not done, but simply because we exist.

That's hard for some Western minds to accept. We are steeped in the notion that every man is ultimately a rational actor. But that's wrong. There is evil in the world, and sometimes it must be confronted, and sometimes that confrontation is going to be violent, and sometimes it is going to lead to war. I wish it weren't that way, but wishing doesn't change reality.

There are countries and groups and individuals in this world who are willing to fight and die for the single purpose of killing Americans. Sometimes a leader needs an enemy, and America is often a convenient one because we're the world's most powerful defender of personal liberty, democracy, and free trade.

But there is a strong current of belief on the Left, and in the current administration, that irrational actors on the world stage are just rational actors in waiting, and that they are reasonable people to whom we just haven't talked enough. This naïve belief often coincides with the convictions that the American experiment is fundamentally unfair, that capitalism hurts the world, and that America deserves whatever insults or attacks befall us.

Republicans know better. Regardless of America's mistakes, we are still the freest nation on earth and offer the greatest promise to those in bondage or without hope. We believe that evil is real, that you always have to be ready to fight it, and that the physical safety of our citizens and our homeland truly is worth fighting for.

National security should not be a game for scoring political points. It should reflect a common purpose and understanding of America's exceptional role in an increasingly dangerous world. Of course, this doesn't mean Democrats and Republicans can't have legitimate differences on foreign policy. But those differences should reflect different *means* to get to the same overall goal: keeping America safe and strong.

Democrats and Republicans, despite often bitter differences, used to agree on one thing: that America is not simply one country among many. Instead, it is something exceptional, with a special role to play in defending freedom around the world. Waging the Cold War was not the domain of just one party. It reflected a national consensus on the danger of Communism. It was a Democrat, President Harry Truman, who laid out the strategy of containment that guided a half-century of U.S. Cold War policy through to victory. While requesting aid from Congress to resist Communist encroachments in Greece and to stabilize Turkey, Truman cited an obligation arising from America's position as leader of the free world:

> The seeds of totalitarian regimes are nurtured by
> misery and want. They spread and grow in the evil

soil of poverty and strife. They reach their full growth when the hope of a people for a better life has died. We must keep that hope alive.

The free peoples of the world look to us for support in maintaining their freedoms.

If we falter in our leadership, we may endanger the peace of the world—and we shall surely endanger the welfare of our own nation.

Today, some Americans seem to have grown weary of this leadership. They don't want to bear the price of defending freedom or withstand the criticism from other countries that our leadership has always encountered. For the eight years of George W. Bush's presidency, many voices at home attacked our military missions, especially in Iraq. Some of these were principled, legitimate criticisms of our mistakes. But others merely sought to exploit a dangerous time to attack a Republican administration by smearing anyone associated with the mission—MoveOn.org's disgraceful advertisement labeling General Petraeus, the architect of the successful troop surge in Iraq, as "General Betray Us" is a prime example.

We need to move on from these debilitating accusations. Republicans and Democrats will continue passionately voicing our differences on foreign policy; unlike most of our enemies, we're not a one-party state. But we should all agree that our foreign policy should be rooted in American exceptionalism—America is not just another country. We are the leader of the free world because we're the only nation that can fill that role.

Unfortunately, President Obama does not seem to think America is all that special. When asked by a reporter in France if he believed in American exceptionalism, our president replied, "I believe in American exceptionalism, just as I suspect that the Brits believe in British exceptionalism and the Greeks believe in Greek exceptionalism." In other words, he doesn't believe in American exceptionalism at all. Obama's feel-good answer turned the notion of American exceptionalism into its exact opposite: he thinks everyone is exceptional—which means no one is exceptional.

The president's rhetoric and his policies reflect a belief—and even a hope—that the world has evolved beyond U.S. dominance. One example is the Obama administration's decision to cede most U.S. control over ICANN—the nonprofit corporation that manages the Internet by controlling the domain name system. Although ICANN has done a fine job, some countries have complained that it's not "fair" that the United States controls it. So President Obama has pushed ICANN toward a new transnational status. While that may please the international political class that Obama is so intent on gratifying, it also makes the Internet more vulnerable to foreign pressures for regulation, taxation, and censorship.

Here's a final example of President Obama's dismissal of American exceptionalism: in his September 2009 address to the UN General Assembly, he proclaimed, "No world order that elevates one nation or group of people over another will succeed." Well, I have some news for the president: America *has* been elevated over other nations. We've been elevated by history, by our emergence in the last century as a superpower, and later, as the only superpower. Whether Obama likes it or not, this places unique responsibilities on us to defend our allies and to promote freedom. He might try to make other countries feel good by pretending we're all equal, but that's not going to make it true. When some international miscreant threatens world peace, the international community doesn't look to Papua New Guinea to take action. When a devastating tsunami, earthquake, or other natural disaster strikes, no one asks Kyrgyzstan for help. They ask us.

Many nations today are free because we secured their freedom and continue to defend it. Nevertheless, some of those same nations are among our loudest critics. This brings to mind President Kennedy's famous inauguration speech in which he vowed to "bear any burden" to defend liberty. That line has rightly become famous, but there's another passage in that speech that is just applicable today as when JFK declared it nearly fifty years ago:

> To those new States whom we welcome to the ranks of the free, we pledge our word that one form of colonial control shall not have passed away merely to be replaced by a far more iron tyranny. We shall not always expect to find them supporting our view. But we shall always hope to find them strongly supporting their own freedom—and to remember that, in the past, those who foolishly sought power by riding the back of the tiger ended up inside.

We defend freedom at home by defending freedom abroad. That is our historic, national consensus, and it should remain so.

THREE

WINNING THE ARGUMENT

President Obama's far-left policies have already failed. We need to expose the damage they're doing and clearly explain our conservative solutions.

STEP

9

Take Back the Culture

AMERICA should be a place where men and women can fully and freely exercise the right to live as they choose, even when others disagree with those choices. That's just what Republicans believe.

Democrats might *say* they want that too, but far more often their policies aim to constrain your personal freedom. Sometimes they do it by outlawing what they don't like, from simple light bulbs to "hate speech." Other times they foreclose on economic opportunity by heaping new regulations on people and businesses, often cynically presenting their restrictions as "more opportunity and choice." And still other times they try to "encourage" you to engage in what they believe to be virtuous behavior, using the government's taxation and subsidizing powers to get you to eat the "right" foods, buy the "right" cars, and the like. Insidiously, through all these mechanisms, they encourage a culture that diminishes and denigrates all but their own moral choices.

Personal morality should be a personal matter, not a government matter, as long as a person's choices do not damage or destroy the lives of others (as abortion does, for instance), or carry crippling social and economic consequences (such as drug use), or interfere with the ability to govern (as the various sex scandals in both parties do).

Liberals have developed their own moral code, however, and they are using all the weapons at their disposal—the news media, the education system, popular entertainment, you name it—to instill it in the rest of us. They seem determined to tear down any remaining vestiges of traditional morality. Their relentless mocking of Christianity, of course, is the prime example. If Hollywood or the *New York Times* treated Islam or other religions with the unconcealed contempt they reserve for Christianity, their own liberal activist allies would be calling for hate crimes prosecutions.

We discussed liberal intolerance before, but it's worth revisiting in the context of the so-called culture war. The ground under this war has changed, and leading Democrats have buried the old notion of "tolerance"—at least when it comes to tolerating traditional values, the practice of Christianity, and the primacy of the nuclear family. They present the cultural foundations of American society less often as ideals to strive for than as rotten pillars of a morally corrupt nation or the butt of vulgar jokes.

Open hostility to traditional morality deeply infects liberalism today, revealing liberals to be far more intolerant than those they criticize. For all their talk about diversity, liberals actively oppose the most important kind of diversity a free society can have: diversity of opinion. They really just regard "tolerance" as a useful rhetorical weapon to flay conservatives for not agreeing with their agenda.

It is time to take back the culture, but in a different way than we have considered before. We should not sit idly by while the Left continues to denigrate traditional moral and religious values. To borrow from the president's playbook, we need to call them out on it. We should point out how their aspersions violate the "tolerance" that liberals uphold as the most sacred of all values. We must argue that there's nothing particularly "liberal" about ridiculing people's religious beliefs. And we need to ask whether the current attack on all things Christian would meet with the approval of yesterday's liberal icons—like the Reverend Martin Luther King Jr.

Too many liberals consider socially conservative values to be beyond the pale of reasonable discussion. Tell a liberal you homeschool your kids, and get ready to be labeled a bigot or a religious nut. And even if you agree with liberals on nearly every issue, declare you are pro-life and you will quickly wear out your welcome.

Traditional values are under withering assault at college campuses across America, where conservative speakers are heckled and even physically attacked—when their invitations to speak haven't been rescinded in the first place. At many universities, the entire press runs of conservative student newspapers have been stolen. Sadly, new examples of liberal intolerance appear every week.

America needs responsible leaders who welcome a vigorous clash of ideas. But Democrats have abandoned even the pretense of listening to dissenting viewpoints. They are shutting down free debate with political correctness, and they've become nearly obsessed with smashing those who think differently than they do. If Democrats are going to tear down a primary pillar of democracy—yes, it really is that serious—then Republicans have to work twice as hard to keep what's left and to restore what's been lost.

Now, some liberals claim Republicans "gave Democrats as good as they got" during the political debates of the last decade— and they are wrong. True, we demanded evidence to back up their wild claims. We criticized protests that opposed everything except terrorism. We called liberals to account for the spurious charges they made against our soldiers.

But we never questioned their right to speak out, and we never tried to silence them.

We never tried to use the law or regulation to take their radio programs off the air.

We never tried to get the FCC to threaten broadcasters with the loss of their licenses.

The Democrats did all these things and more. Not us.

Many Democrats think all's fair in shutting down their opponents, but that's not true. Politics isn't a football game where you cheer for the winner and boo the cross-town rival and forget all about it at the party afterward. Political choices have lasting impact in determining how—and how well—we live. For the sake of the generations of Americans who will come after us, there are some lines you do not cross.

What's more, it is not enough simply to satisfy the letter of the law. The spirit of America is the spirit of open debate and respect for your opponent's right to free speech, even if you detest his or her ideas. Democrats won't always be in power, and someday they will need the same tolerance for their ideas that they diminish for others today. But if their example sticks, that safe harbor will be gone when they will need it most.

Republicans should remind Americans at every opportunity that what Democrats call tolerance is really a license to read traditional values out of the public square, while demanding our moral approval of every behavior under the sun—even those that the vast majority find perverse and offensive. The penalty for stating, even in a civil, courteous way, that you prefer traditional or socially conservative values is to be labeled a bigot or worse—as former Miss California Carrie Prejean discovered when she gave the "wrong" answer at a beauty pageant to a question about gay marriage. After simply expressing her belief in traditional marriage, Prejean endured a torrent of abuse from across the liberal spectrum, with the pageant judge who asked her the question, Perez Hilton, later calling her an unprintable expletive and condemning her answer as "the worst in pageant history."

Liberal intolerance is not just a matter of hurt feelings or being "left out." It can have ramifications for getting or keeping a job, being accepted to college, passing or failing a class, and more. It's a serious matter. Republicans are on the right side of this. And the Democrats are indefensibly wrong.

For years I've heard liberals try to win over low-income and minority voters with the vague promise of "hope." Like you, I've heard it all: Jesse Jackson pleading, "Keep hope alive!"; Bill Clinton calling himself "the man from a place called Hope"; and Barack Obama promising "the audacity of hope"—a phrase that seems to mean whatever he decides it means at any given moment.

"Hope" is an easy sell, because anybody can make promises. But hope improves lives only when it is transformed into reality, and that requires action.

As Republicans, our mission today is the same as it was when the Grand Old Party was founded in 1854: to empower people— even the powerless—to bring their hopes into reality. Empty rhetoric won't do it, no matter how catchy and popular. It takes hard work—especially when political leaders show real leadership by doing the right thing when it's not easy to do. We are the party of Abraham Lincoln, and the Great Emancipator took a stand for those whose hands and feet were literally shackled.

Today's Republicans must stand with those who find themselves shackled by new chains: lack of education, lack of opportunity, and most important, lack of knowledge about how they can participate in the American system and make a better life for themselves and their families.

The liberals had their chance and they have failed in tragic, heartless ways. After the civil rights movement of the 1960s, American history should have been a story of triumph and rapid progress for minorities, and especially for African-Americans. Instead, liberals assumed they could simply legislate compassion, mandate acceptance, and everything for black Americans would turn around.

They were wrong.

Human experience teaches that real change must first take root in our hearts, and hearts change by choice, not by force. Law alone is insufficient; it takes the constant and good example of men and women who do the right thing because they want to, not because they have to. The liberals' lack of this basic appreciation for how societies change has led directly to the creation of a perpetual underclass populated by the neediest Americans. Our fellow citizens have been trapped there in part by the refusal of liberals to require even the simplest of moral compasses of themselves and others.

As an African-American man, when I consider how liberals have deigned to excuse ignorance, illegitimacy, and vulgarity as artifacts of black America's "culture"; when I recall how they have made common cause with self-appointed, race-hustling "spokesmen" who make a living by feeding racial conflict, not fighting it; when I see the old "white man's burden" dressed up as liberal *noblesse oblige*—when I see all that against generations of young black men in prison and generations of young black women raising babies all alone, I raise my fists in righteous anger.

People in need deserve to know how America works—that they can get a degree, learn a skill, or start a business and get ahead. Opportunity is not the province of wealth and privilege alone. It is available to everyone, and it is their right as Americans to take advantage of it—but few people show them how.

Instead, they hear over and over that America has made them victims. This starts with what children are taught in public schools: in history class, social studies, and even in ostensibly non-political subjects like math, there is a persistent message— sometimes subtle, other times quite open—that America is little more than an arena for the struggle of oppressed groups. Every- one is a victim—including *you*. And since life's hardships aren't your fault, don't make it your responsibility to overcome them. Find someone to blame, then demand they do the heavy lifting. History is a cast around your legs and a chain around your feet. You are at the mercy of powers beyond your control, and the only reason you have less is that others have more.

We must replace that liberal lie with the truth. Success comes only when we stop feeling sorry for ourselves, stop bellyaching about our circumstances, accept reality for what it is, and use our talents to the best of our abilities.

Is that fair? No. It's not fair that some people are poorer than others, and our society needs to maintain an effective safety net for those who fall through the cracks. But government attempts to *mandate* equality never work—they result in social leveling that degrades the incentive to work hard and start businesses. Under those conditions, a lot of people become poorer, while the poor don't become any wealthier—they only become less free. In fact, the only ones who become better off are members of the governing class.

It is no coincidence that the most economically free countries and territories—America, Hong Kong, Great Britain, Singapore, New Zealand, Switzerland, and Chile, to name a few—tend to have high living standards and high per capita income. At a time when even Communist countries like China and Vietnam are moving toward economic freedom, we should resist exhortations to move in the opposite direction in hopes of achieving some utopian state of equality.

So life may not be fair, but wallowing in your supposed victimhood is a surefire route to a bitter, unhappy, unsuccessful life. Wait for "fairness" to rescue you from difficulty and you'll be waiting a long, long time. Meanwhile, life is going to pass you by. You'll never get ahead until you start playing the hand you're dealt. The American way—hard work and helping your family and your community—really works. It'll get you ahead.

Pursing the American dream might not make you a millionaire, but most Americans who embrace hard work and self-reliance at least achieve what the vast majority of the world only dreams of: a place to live that they can call their own, some money in the bank, and the satisfaction of making a life for themselves and their family in safety and comfort.

Being an American means you can write your own future. It doesn't matter where you start, as long as you understand that nothing good comes overnight, setbacks are part of moving forward, and there is no substitute for perseverance and self-discipline. It won't be easy—no good thing ever is. But knowledge is a powerful thing, and Republicans are committed to making sure every American knows how to take advantage of the opportunities our system affords.

Liberals see America as an acid stew of bigotry, historic offense, and unchecked individualism. Most Americans—and most people around the world who want to come here—find that bizarre. People know America is not perfect, but most are far more excited at the possibility—the "hope," to put that word in its proper context—that America presents to anyone who reaches out for it. America is where you come when you want tomorrow to be better for your children than today is for you.

Republicans know what America really has to offer, and so do people around the world.

———————————

While providing a safety net, the government should seek to elevate those in need to overcome government dependence—yet one of President Obama's first acts was to pay the states to expand their welfare rolls. And that gives you some idea of just what we're up against: the Democrats' idea of success is to make more families dependent on government.

Opportunity and education are critical, but those things alone can't cure the hardest cases. Sometimes we have to reach out and help each other—and the last half-century of history shows that government is too big, too clumsy, and too impersonal to offer real compassion. We have to do it ourselves, as human obligation. When we start caring about each other as neighbors and as fellow members of our communities—something Democrats could learn from the religious conservatives they ridicule—we will improve the life of the most disadvantaged Americans far more powerfully than a government check can.

The light of America is its promise of endless possibilities. She truly is "a shining city on a hill," as President Reagan put it. That city must have a place for everyone, no matter where they come from, and no matter how high they intend to climb.

But what liberals often forget is that it's not the government that makes that city shine. It is the people. What makes the difference for the family on the brink of poverty or prosperity is not government; it is the people. It is the people, not the government, who will raise up those suffering the dehumanizing effects of poverty and addiction—caught in hopelessness that is carried from one generation to the next like an infection across the heart. They deserve the benefits of freedom and free enterprise as much as anyone, and it will be the people of America who will bring that new day, not government.

Like Reagan, I put my faith in people, not government. Like Lincoln, I "declare for liberty." It is morning in America, still, because America *is* morning. America is a place of eternal promise and potential, a place where possibility meets opportunity, a place where the son of a sharecropper's daughter can realize dreams his ancestors never even dared to dream and can help fulfill the promise of a great nation.

STEP

10

Take Back the Economy

SPEAKER of the House Nancy Pelosi, Senate Majority Leader Harry Reid, and President Obama are exploiting Americans' economic fears to justify policies designed to unravel the familiar fabric of American life. The scale of their agenda is truly breathtaking, and they will not be stopped by any inconvenient economic reality—like the fact that the country can't afford what they want to do. With significant parts of our banking and automotive industries already lying in government hands, the

Democrats now have their sights set on America's healthcare system and energy industries.

The American people know what's going on, and our response has been a resounding "No More!" In townhall meetings, public opinion surveys, and every other available medium, Americans have demanded the government stop its out-of-control spending and borrowing. But without an election in the immediate future, public demands don't interest the Democrats very much. In fact, what passes for a response has been dismissive or outright insulting. In light of the Democrats' arrogant disdain for all dissent, the new "post-partisan" era we were promised sure looks a lot like the old partisan one.

The policies we've seen out of both ends of Pennsylvania Avenue represent an arrogance of power and some of the most reckless spending, borrowing, and taxing America has ever seen, with numerous broken promises thrown in for good measure. With the Democratic Congress acting as little more than a rubber stamp for President Obama's agenda of governmental gigantism, the liberals' brief time in office has already produced massive new debt, rising unemployment, the specter of inflation, a weakening dollar, and a new raft of suffocating regulations on businesses.

Is this the "change" America voted for? First came the Democrats' $787 billion "stimulus" package. The stimulus was effective in exactly one thing: handing out billions of dollars in pork-barrel spending without creating new jobs. Then came the $410 billion omnibus spending bill that contained *eight thousand* earmarks. President Obama signed it, even though he promised during the campaign that he would "go line by line through every item in the federal budget and eliminate programs that don't work and make sure that those that do work, work better and cheaper."

Of course, he also promised that the public would have five days to examine bills online before he signed them. Oops—guess he didn't really mean that one either. Out of the first eleven bills he signed into law, he kept his promise for transparency on only one of them. The public was given less than a day to read the 1,100-page stimulus bill before the House voted on it. The same goes for the 1,200-page Waxman-Markey global warming bill. Later, we were given less than three days to read the massive, 2,000-page healthcare bill. Essentially, it was impossible for anyone—including congressmen—to read these entire bills before they were approved. That's not transparency—that's bamboozling the American people.

But the Great Obama Spending Spree wasn't over—as Al Pacino might say, he was just getting warmed up. Next came the president's jaw-dropping $3.6 trillion budget that would raise taxes on the very job-producing small businesses our economy needs right now. According to the Congressional Budget Office, planned federal spending will require an additional *$9 trillion* in borrowing over the next ten years. This is a crushing debt being tied around the necks of our children and grandchildren, leaving them in hock to China and other countries for generations to come. How much is $9 trillion worth?

- about $100,000 for every working family
- about $30,000 for every man, woman, and child
- almost fifty times the value of the Wal-Mart corporation

- more than seventy times the cost of the entire effort to put a man on the moon
- more than three times higher than the highest federal budget under a Republican president

Or look at $9 trillion this way: it's about two-thirds of U.S. Gross Domestic Product (GDP)—the value of all goods and services produced in one year.

But no matter how you look at $9 trillion in debt, remember this: it stems from Democratic spending plans. Congressional Republicans offered to work with the president on bipartisan solutions, only to be shut out of the process by Nancy Pelosi and other Democrats. The budget passed under the direct leadership of Pelosi, Harry Reid, and Barack Obama—only they're not going to pay for it. It is going to be paid by you and me and our children, and our grandchildren, and their children's children.

Unsurprisingly, Obama has asked the Senate to raise the federal debt ceiling beyond $12.1 trillion. It's funny, when President Bush asked the Senate to raise the debt ceiling to facilitate his own lavish spending, then Senator Obama denounced the president as an irresponsible spendthrift. "Washington is shifting the burden of bad choices today onto the backs of our children and grandchildren," Obama declared shortly before voting against Bush's request. Now that Obama's the one who's doing the spending, however, he's suddenly a lot less worried about placing our children in debt.

Republicans understand that maximizing our resources to get our economy back on track is our top priority right now. This is where we diverge from the Democrats. We don't believe that mortgaging this country's economic future with mindboggling borrowing and spending is a good way to fight the recession. We don't think wasting taxpayer dollars on dollops of special interest pork is a good way to fight the recession. We don't think foisting a debilitating energy tax on American industry and consumers in the form of a "cap-and-trade" system is a good way to fight the recession. And we don't think blowing billions of taxpayer dollars to subsidize the creation of useless, needless "green jobs" is a good way to fight the recession.

The most obvious expression of voter frustration with these out-of-control spending policies was the proliferation of "tea parties" across America beginning around Tax Day in April 2009. These were true grassroots events attended by deeply-concerned Americans, yet Pelosi and the Left dismissed them as irrelevant. The liberal media, which is so enthralled by far-left protest that it turned Cindy Sheehan into a national celebrity, suddenly found protesting to be worthy of ridicule. Allegedly "serious" liberal commentators such as CNN's Anderson Cooper, MSNBC's Rachel Maddow and David Shuster, and *Time* magazine's Ana Marie Cox found a crude double-meaning in the phrase "tea bag" and giggled through a parade of sex jokes about Americans who dared to call for responsible spending policies.

The contempt shown by liberal elites toward the protestors did not take many conservatives by surprise, but the hypocrisy never fails to impress. President Obama reacted to the furor with a hollow gesture that was good for some additional fawning media coverage—the only kind he ever gets. The president sternly requested members of his cabinet to trim $100 million in spending out of his $4 trillion budget. Dollar for dollar, this is equivalent to asking a family earning $40,000 a year to give up a single dollar. Even the *Washington Post* ridiculed Obama's request, saying it was "like trying to deal with a $5,000 credit card debt by forgoing a pack of gum."

A few months later, Democrats in townhall meetings were forced to answer to angry citizens for their support of Obama's healthcare plan. Pelosi and other liberal leaders whined that their opponents were unruly "mobs," and that people who disagreed with Obama's plan were unworthy of having their questions answered. In a piece in *USA Today*, Pelosi and Democratic House majority leader Steny Hoyer even called the healthcare protestors "un-American." Other Democrats reacted with fear—some were so afraid of answering the opponents of Obama's healthcare scheme that they cancelled townhalls altogether.

Although we Republicans will continue to oppose this administration's irresponsible economic schemes and spending policies, I'll give the Democrats credit where it's due: President Obama's decision not to reopen negotiations of the North American Free Trade Agreement (NAFTA) was the right one for America's economy and for our relations with our Canadian and Latin American neighbors.

Of course, he broke his campaign promises when he made that decision—but I'm glad he did. This reversal from far-left policy is a fleeting exception to a dangerous liberal agenda, the cornerstone of which is more spending and more borrowing. The American people hope for better from the president, the speaker, and congressional Democrats—but we've learned not to expect it.

President Obama is a man of charm and charisma. Though his stature has already diminished, his election-year rhetoric resonated with Americans struggling to make ends meet. The electoral landscape in 2008 was tailor-made for a man offering optimism instead of detail—he campaigned on equal parts audacity and vacuous promises of "hope." Concerns over his inexperience in both domestic policy and national security were overwhelmed by the man's exceptional ability to be all things to all people. Oh, and he can give a pretty good speech too.

Americans saw what they wanted to see in Barack Obama and discounted the parts they didn't like as unimportant. He became a human Rorschach Test for a nation looking to turn the page on a divisive era—even though it was the most obstinate members of Barack Obama's party who made it that way.

As the country looks to emerge from the burst housing bubble, financial market turmoil, and the overall recession, we need steady, responsible economic leadership. The economic crisis is just that—a crisis. It's not an "opportunity" to ram through transformative policies that seek to re-shape America from top to bottom. Because the administration used the crisis for that purpose, however, the public's fascination with Obama's fresh face and mellifluous voice is giving way, less than a year into his presidency, to a growing realization that a president's lofty rhetoric and "rock star" status may be entertaining, but they won't get anyone a job, put gas in anyone's car, or keep food on anyone's table.

Obama called for "middle class" tax relief during his campaign, but that promise was DOA, replaced by punitive taxes on those who otherwise would spend that money to create jobs and invest in an economy that badly needs private-sector help. Although reducing the capital gains tax would expand economic opportunities for the most economically disadvantaged workers by bringing jobs and new businesses to capital-starved areas such as America's inner cities, President Obama wants to raise the tax.

His reasoning: "I would look at raising the capital gains tax for purposes of fairness."

Note that with that sentence, President Obama dismisses the *effect* of tax hikes on the economy. Tax hikes may be economically damaging, but that's not what concerns him. What concerns him is *fairness*—some people are making more money than others, and that's not fair. His true goal, without doubt, is the redistribution of wealth. Since he made this quite clear more than once during his campaign, we really should not be surprised.

In Obama's world, the government gets to pick winners and losers, micro-managing the economy so that the "right" amount of wealth goes to the "right" people and places. Obama hopes to continue fooling the American people into believing that a tax on business is not a tax on all of us. But what a naïve thing for the leader of the free world to believe! You don't need a degree in rocket science to realize that "businesses" don't pay "business taxes" any more than your house pays property taxes. Every tax is ultimately paid by some person as a percentage of the wages they earn. Taxes "on business" are just passed along in the form of higher prices, fewer new jobs, and less business expansion.

When President Obama calls for increasing taxes on "big business," it's a call for increased taxes on the backs of hard-working wage earners. He pretends not to know that, but he really does. And you do too.

One of the more economically damaging aspects of the current liberal agenda is energy policy. The high energy prices we saw in 2008 were a dream come true for liberals. In fact, President

Obama is so blinded by environmental extremism that he spoke out during his campaign *in support* of higher gas prices. In June 2008, as gasoline was approaching record-setting prices of more than $4.00 a gallon, then candidate Obama told CNBC that high gas prices aren't so bad—they had merely gone up too fast, and he "would have preferred a gradual adjustment."

Okay, so liberals say that high gas prices could be beneficial if they encourage us to shake off our dependence on foreign oil. Well then, what about increasing our own oil supply? Surely Democrats can agree with Republicans that replacing foreign oil with American oil is a good thing, right?

Wrong.

When Senate Republicans proposed opening domestic exploration to lessen our dependence on foreign oil, the Democratic majority blocked not just a vote on the measure but even any discussion of it. As Senator Mitch McConnell noted at the time, "It's as if [the Democrats] are doing everything in their power to keep gas prices from going down."

Now what could possibly give that impression? Could it be that Democrats and liberals have blocked nearly every initiative to drill for new oil anywhere in America? Drilling off-shore, drilling in Alaska, drilling for oil shale in Colorado's Green River Formation—all stymied by liberals. That's because liberals aren't really worried about our dependence on foreign oil. Increasingly carried away by global warming alarmism, they now largely oppose *all* use of oil and other fossil fuels, regardless of where it came from, simply as a matter of ideology.

If you think President Obama stands apart from such wrongheaded environmental extremism, think again. He appointed

Steven Chu as his Secretary of Energy—and Chu is on record in no uncertain terms about where he wants gas prices: sky-high. "Somehow we have to figure out how to boost the price of gasoline to the levels in Europe," Chu told the *Wall Street Journal* in September 2008. At the time, the price of gas in Europe ranged from $8 to $9 a gallon.

When it comes to blowing up the price of energy, liberals don't let a little thing like hardship for families stand in the way. Jay Hakes, an alumnus of both the Carter and Clinton administrations, told the *Wall Street Journal* that "[t]here's no way we can create a better future without the price of [fossil-fuel-based] energy going up. But it's tough for a politician to get up and say 'Your prices are going to have to go up.'"

The debate about energy has been anything but a debate. For the Left, it's been more about demonizing oil, natural gas, and coal as energy sources, and about thoroughly misrepresenting the potential of offshore drilling. Democrats have especially focused on attacking oil companies as devious, greedy, and rapacious forces of evil, while blocking every attempt to open new American wells. What's even more insulting is the Obama administration's decision to lend $2 billion to Brazil's state-owned oil company to drill for oil off Brazil's coast. The president finally passed a measure that will actually create jobs, and it turns out they're all in South America.

Democrats pay lip service to making America energy independent, but when it comes to actual policy, they oppose the expansion of nearly every type of energy. Conventional oil, oil shale, coal, natural gas, nuclear power—they've all been stymied by over-regulation and never-ending lawsuits by environmental groups designed to impede *any* expansion of the energy supply. The only energy sources they can abide are "green" sources like wind and solar. These sources, even after enjoying decades of government subsidies, only comprise around 1 percent of the U.S. energy supply. Despite the utopian promises of a "green economy," they could never come close to satisfying America's energy needs.

But the American people know better. When we say "Drill, baby, drill!" we say it for a reason: we want a comprehensive energy policy that utilizes the latest technologies and produces more oil, natural gas, and coal, develops nuclear as well as renewable sources, and ultimately achieves energy independence.

In line with his party's inexplicable crusade against our own country's oil companies, President Obama has voiced support for slapping a "windfall" profits tax on them. Those taxes, of course, would simply get passed along to consumers at the pump—and President Obama knows it. This is just one more chapter in the Obama playbook to "spread the wealth around," as he characterized it, and it has nothing to do with improving America's energy situation. Democrats want to limit domestic exploration even if it leaves us dependent on anti-American states around the globe, and the president advocates further hamstringing the market with even more suffocating regulation.

Republicans have a better answer. We want to expand our domestic energy supply and reform the federal policies that drive up gas prices. What's more, we want you to know the truth about gas prices: as much as a third of the price at the pump is taxes. Gas that's $3.00 a gallon could be $2.00 a gallon if the government wasn't taking a cut every time you fill up your tank.

On free trade, Republicans believe that the best way to ensure long-term growth and prosperity is to encourage economic liberty—the foundation of our free-market system—by lowering global trade barriers and making it easier for domestic industries to thrive in the global marketplace. A different view is held by President Obama, who engaged in a lot of old-fashioned demagoguery of free trade on the campaign trail, especially in pivotal states such as Michigan, Pennsylvania, Ohio, and Minnesota. At the time unemployment was on the rise in those states, making attacks on free trade more popular.

At first, it was hard to tell whether the president's broadsides against free trade were just political posturing—his belated acceptance of NAFTA offered some hope that he'd champion free markets. But his true outlook has now become clear: he slapped a 35 percent tariff on imports of Chinese tires, provoking predictable threats of retaliation from the Chinese; he has allowed progress to stall on numerous free trade agreements, including crucial ones with South Korean and Columbia; and he included an array of protectionist provisions in the stimulus.

President Obama's bent for protectionism contradicts a rare point of agreement among mainstream economists—that free trade brings prosperity at home and abroad. Yet Obama spreads the false promise among people in economic hardship that throwing up barriers to free trade is somehow the key to all our problems. To the contrary, free trade is a vital source of economic growth, especially during a recession. The last thing we want now is to instigate a new bout of worldwide protectionism like the one witnessed in 1930, which was a key contributor to the Great Depression.

Protectionism has been so discredited that it is now less an economically justifiable position than a transparent excuse for paying off well-heeled special interests, especially union bosses and environmental extremists, by placing draconian limits on our ability to buy and sell with other nations.

The sluggish U.S. economy would be even worse were it not for increases in U.S. exports enabled by Republicans who fought for free trade. According to the U.S. Department of Commerce, exports accounted for almost two-thirds of our nation's economic growth last year, providing an especially needed boon for small businesses. Those small businesses are the backbone of the American economy, and we need to appreciate the vital contribution they make to our communities. Most important, we need to preserve and expand their ability to trade freely with the rest of the world. Protectionist policies may please certain special interests, but they ultimately bring two main results: job losses and higher prices.

There is no magic potion for moving this economy in a new direction. But Republican policies stand in stark contrast to those of President Obama.

We empower citizens. President Obama and his liberal friends empower government. Republicans trust individuals to make their own decisions—as employees, as business owners, as savers, as investors, and as Americans "endowed with certain unalienable rights" to live life as we choose. Obama trusts the coercive power of government to make more and more deci-sions—economic and otherwise—that most Americans believe should be left to the individual.

Economic policies should be geared toward empowering businesses so they can expand and create new opportunities for workers and investors. That is the path to "legacy wealth"— getting families out of poverty, public assistance, or mere suste-nance, and helping them discover the power of financial responsibility and independence, so they set a good example for future generations.

In the end, a strong economy means a better quality of life for the people of the United States. Our families, friends and loved ones can look forward to increased stability, successful communities, and a brighter future—but not as long as those who run the government insist on running everything else, too.

Hope is a wonderful thing. It can inspire us to achieve more than we dreamed was possible. It can be the catalyst for action out of inaction, and the inspiration for moving beyond indecision. Hope is the thing that helps us discover our higher, better selves.

Hope is our reaction to reality. It is not an alternative to real-ity. And it is not policy.

Lots of people are impressed by charisma and personality, but novelty never lasts forever. Like a one-hit wonder on the radio, President Obama and the liberals in the House and Senate are learning this lesson the hard way and leaving us to foot the bill. What remains of the president's popularity is proving an ineffec-tive weapon to distract the American people from the reality that liberals are offering the same old heavy-handed, nanny-state economic policies that Americans have rejected time after time.

Liberals believe Obama's lyrical expressions and personal popularity will allow them to get away with anything, but they're wrong. If the American people didn't like deficits under Republican leadership, they're not going to like them any more under a Democrat—especially when the taxing and borrowing and spending greatly exceeds any previous U.S. budget.

The Obama administration's eagerness to vastly expand the federal government's role in the economy is disturbing. What's more, it's extremely arrogant. The government is now running car companies and choosing their CEOs. But does the government really have the necessary expertise to run these companies successfully? You'll notice there's not a line of business leaders stretching around the White House volunteering to let our self-appointed business guru, Barack Obama, make their decisions for them. That's because they know Obama never dealt with a payroll, never did inventory, and never had employees depend on him to keep a business open and profitable so they could continue working there. Also, unlike the president, America's business leaders understand the proper role of government.

Most Americans know where our rights begin and end—unlike liberals, who believe their influence, and their access to taxpayer money, is limited only by their imaginations.

We can do better. Republicans must present better ideas that acknowledge our responsibility not to saddle future generations with unsustainable debt. Most important, we need to stand up for American enterprise, since the Democrats no longer will. Businesses are not out to get us, oil companies are not the source of all our woes, and earning a profit is no cause for shame. We should proudly stand for free markets and free people—two crucial elements of America's historic rise to greatness.

STEP

11

Take Back National Security

WHEN IT COMES to foreign policy and national security, America's leaders should always focus on one task above all others: preserving the safety of Americans. Other considerations of both foreign and domestic policy are secondary—every one of them. If we aren't safe here at home, what is the point of doing anything else?

Republicans know that sound foreign policy must directly address an unpleasant truth: America has dangerous enemies, and some of them want to kill us. Of course, some people don't believe

that at all, insisting that terrorism directed against us is only the
United States reaping what she has sown. (In fact, a lot of those
folks work in the White House right now.) With a few exceptions,
such as Senator Joe Lieberman, Democrats claim Republicans are
"fear-mongering" for recognizing the evil forces arrayed against
us. Unsurprisingly, Lieberman is no longer officially a Democrat.

Most Democratic leaders see the world as they wish it were,
and that is profoundly dangerous—like driving down a windy
road with your eyes closed and imagining a straight path. Republicans understand that to capably defend America and its interests, you have to understand the world as it really is. That's
challenging, because the notion that America has irredeemable
enemies goes against the spirit of American optimism—the belief
so many of us have, deep down, that everyone in the world wants
to get along with each other, and especially with us. We like to be
liked—Obama won the presidency in part on his insistence that
our national security challenges stem from the international
unpopularity of President Bush. The mere election of "beloved"
Obama, we were led to believe, would turn enemies into friends
and make us all safer.

But being liked doesn't make peace—being respected makes
peace. And being strong makes peace—remember President
Reagan's policy of "peace through strength"? To be respected
and strong, you have to stand up for a few things, and stand
against a whole lot of others. Republicans—and the vast majority of Americans—are willing to do that, but our current com-
mander in chief is not.

President Obama has done some good things in foreign policy, especially reversing his campaign promise to quickly withdraw

all U.S. forces from Iraq, which would have left a fledgling democracy exposed to threats from within and from abroad. But after less than a year of his presidency, it's already become clear that certain policies don't increase our strength, international respect, or security. Those policies include:

- going around the world apologizing for defending ourselves
- palling around with thuggish left-wing dictators like Hugo Chavez, accepting their propaganda books as gifts, and shaking hands and smiling with them for the camera
- dithering about whether to fulfill his generals' requests to send more troops into Afghanistan
- trying to halt development on Iran's nuclear weapons program by nicely asking the Iranian regime to stop it
- writing off Iranian freedom fighters in a bid to curry favor with the mad mullahs who oppress them
- prioritizing international opinion over national security by declaring our intention to move terrorists out of Guantanamo Bay and into the United States

To Republicans, this is all common sense.

The twenty-first century requires not only clear thinking about the world, but also a whole new way of approaching the intricacies of foreign policy. We must remain prepared for conventional wars, but we must be equally ready to prevent domestic terrorism and other non-traditional attacks. The horrific massacre of U.S. soldiers at Fort Hood serves as a reminder of the dangers we face. And so does the recent string of terror-related arrests throughout America: jihadists are suspected of plotting to blow up a Dallas skyscraper and a federal building in Springfield, Illinois; planning to attack the New York City subway system and the Marine Corps base in Quantico, Virginia; and attempting to organize killing sprees at Massachusetts shopping malls. The 2009 convictions of four British Islamic extremists for a plot to blow up seven U.S.- and Canada-bound airliners also provide a stark indication of the determination and ruthlessness of our enemies.

If you think we are no longer threatened by terrorism, think again. And terrorists, for some reason, don't seem susceptible to our president's charms.

President George W. Bush ordered two major military operations, in Afghanistan and Iraq, to replace authoritarian regimes with democratic ones. He was often overwhelmed by political opposition, and many Democrats disingenuously portrayed the safety his policies secured for us as evidence that there was no threat at all. Not every one of his policies was perfect, but his principles were right on the mark. Above all else, he understood that America becomes more secure when the world becomes more free.

Earlier, I talked about the vital necessity of promoting self-government and democracy in the context of America's 50-year political, military, and economic struggle to defeat Communism. This kind of grand policy was needed to face down that challenge.

But standing up for liberty doesn't always require guns or even foreign aid. Much of the time, we simply need to tell the world that we're on the side of freedom fighters when those people ask for our support. This is not only a primary step toward spreading democracy, but also a powerful way to build stability so there are fewer problems that drag us into war. This is the most efficient kind of self-defense. It costs us little and reduces the likelihood of military action, with its terrible loss of life and stunning financial toll.

That's why it's a tragedy that Obama has abandoned the long American tradition of speaking out for dissidents resisting totalitarian rule. Take Iran for example. The so-called "Islamic Revolution" of 1979 established Iran as one of the leading terror-sponsoring dictatorships in the world. It began in the impotence of the Jimmy Carter presidency, when Iranian Islamic extremists seized more than fifty American hostages and held them for 444 days. Since then, the mullahs have made hostages of a whole generation of their own people. They have financed terrorism throughout the Middle East, taught their schoolchildren that the Holocaust is a hoax, undermined every attempt at peace between Israel and the Palestinians, and fomented violent attacks against U.S. troops in Iraq. Most crucial, they are now trying to cement their domination of the Middle East by developing a nuclear weapons program.

Containing the Iranian mullahs and their nuclear weapons program is one of America's biggest foreign policy challenges. Briefly, in 2009, it appeared we might get help from the Iranian people themselves. When Iranian president Mahmoud Ahmadinejad and his mullah puppet-masters attempted to steal an election, the Iranian people, weary of decades of oppression, took to the streets in protest. After thirty years of brutality, corruption, and misrule, Iranians seemed poised to overthrow their repressive regime and move toward freedom and perhaps even regional peace. Galvanized, Western leaders praised the protestors' bravery.

Except for President Obama, that is. During those critical days, our president couldn't spare a word of encouragement for the protestors. It was the first opportunity in a generation to destroy Iranian totalitarianism and overthrow one of the world's greatest enemies of peace. It was an opportunity to stabilize the region without putting a single new U.S. soldier on the ground or spending a single additional penny of American tax dollars. But instead of siding openly and proudly with the oppressed Iranian people, President Obama minimized their cause, warning that the difference between the maniacal Iranian president and the protestors' leader, Mir-Houssein Mousavi, "may not be as great as has been advertised."

President Obama could have easily helped and inspired the dissidents, even with a mere casual remark of support. But he would not. Men and women were being gunned down for speaking out for peace and self-government, yet their sacrifice was breezily dismissed by the man who vowed, "We are the change we've been waiting for."

In response to widespread anger at President Obama's position and images of the Iranian regime's bloody crackdown against the protestors, Obama later made a few polite statements asking the regime to respect freedom of speech. His spokesman explained the president's reluctance to back the protestors by claiming Obama was afraid the regime would exploit his comments to tar the protestors as American stooges. The regime did this anyway, of course, but Obama didn't seem to mind—his priority through the entire episode was to avoid angering the Iranian regime in hopes the mullahs would agree, under the benevolent force of Obama's magnetic personality, to abandon their nuclear program.

I wish the president good luck with that, but I'm not holding my breath for the mullahs suddenly to see the error of their ways. Despite Obama's "restraint" as the regime brutally crushed its own people, the mullahs are moving full-speed ahead with their nuclear program, rejecting every proposal from the president for a deal to end their nuclear program. In fact, after nine months of "reaching out" to the mullahs, the only reaction President Obama has gotten from the Iranians is their acknowledgment that they've been secretly working on a *second* nuclear plant.

Meanwhile, as they were cut down in the streets, the brave Iranian people were left without any meaningful sign of support from the world's strongest democracy. But it's even worse than that: as part of its mullah-outreach program, the Obama administration cut off funding for the Iran Human Rights Documentation Center. For five years, this group has catalogued the vicious human rights abuses that the Iranian regime routinely commits against its own people. But these revelations are, shall we say, an inconvenient truth for Obama. So his State Department canceled funding for the center, which is now slated to close down in spring 2010.

Iranians and other people peacefully resisting oppression are the real "change we have been waiting for." To them, "hope" and "change" aren't slogans, cheers, or election-year chants; they are real goals for which they risk their lives. And they deserve to know we're on their side.

In early November 2009, Iranian regime thugs once again beat peaceful protestors in the streets. It was the thirtieth anniversary of the 1979 U.S. embassy takeover, and the mullahs orchestrated their usual anti-American demonstrations. But this time pro-Western demonstrators turned up who, instead of chanting the regime-approved "Death to America" slogans, voiced regret for the hostage-taking and criticized the mullahs. The assault on these demonstrators once again drew hardly any condemnation from Obama. As two Iranian democracy activists wrote in the *Wall Street Journal*, "In regressive realpolitik fashion, [the Obama administration] has grown increasingly reticent about the Iranian people's struggle for human rights, apparently viewing it as irrelevant to U.S. security interests. Rather than bolstering the opposition at a time when the Iranian regime is at its weakest, America is pursing a policy of appeasement."

Liberals aren't criticizing President Obama's weak support for the Iranian protestors, either. That, sadly, is unsurprising. Liberals are utterly disconnected from what's outside their coffee shops and classrooms. They think the world beyond the U.S. is a big debating society. American politics may be a battle of words, but much of the world still fights those battles with guns and tanks. Liberals seem to imagine that dissidents simply show up on the streets of Tehran and pass out flyers, then adjourn to Starbucks to complain about how everything is George Bush's fault. But here again, Democrats are wrong. For people under the boot of oppression, this is real life. And sometimes it's real death.

Republicans know that if those yearning for freedom can fight their own battles today, American soldiers won't have to fight them tomorrow.

The Democrats' refusal to stand up for the Iranian protestors was part of this administration's embrace of a new "realism" in foreign policy. America has a bad history in many parts of the world, we are told, and we should no longer "meddle" in other nations' affairs.

If that's true, it was strange to see President Obama abandon his "hands off" approach in an effort to reinstate a lawless, former Honduran president who has become a *cause célèbre* among Fidel Castro and other luminaries of the extreme Left.

Shortly after the Iranian "election," Honduran president Manuel Zelaya, a leftist ally of Hugo Chavez, was arrested on orders of the Honduran Supreme Court, which was acting on a request by that nation's attorney general. Zelaya, nearing the end of his term, had been organizing a referendum on holding a constitutional convention whose purpose was clearly to eliminate the Honduran Constitution's one-term limit on the presidency. Although both the Honduran Congress and the courts declared the referendum illegal, Zelaya insisted on holding it anyway. Deciding to uphold the law, the Supreme Court ordered the military to arrest Zelaya, who was sent into exile.

Strangely, in response President Obama abandoned his vaunted doctrine of non-interference. Ignoring Zelaya's abuse of power and the Supreme Court's constitutional role in removing him, Obama vehemently denounced the "coup" and insisted that Zelaya be returned to power. To show that it meant business, the administration suspended some U.S. foreign aid to Honduras and even ordered the U.S. embassy to stop granting visas to many Honduran citizens. When the new Honduran government announced plans to hold a new presidential election, the Obama administration threatened not to recognize it unless Zelaya was restored to power first. Think about that: America refused to approve a democratic election unless it was presided over by a leftist strongman who had been legally removed from office by his own country's Supreme Court for abuse of power.

Under U.S. pressure, the Hondurans recently agreed to restore Zelaya to serve the last few months of his term, but this deal already looks ready to collapse. Regardless of the outcome, Obama's inexplicable support for an anti-democratic ally of Hugo Chavez is a strange policy that supports neither democracy nor U.S. interests.

Many Americans want to give President Obama the benefit of the doubt, but he keeps doing things that leave us scratching our heads. There is a pattern, however, in his damaging foreign policy decisions, and it's not keeping us out of other nations' affairs. It's expediency—the expediency of keeping the status quo, no matter how cruel, over the risks of change. Helping people to win freedom from corrupt or oppressive governments is not easy or certain. It takes sustained, dedicated leadership, and it may anger some on the international Left who will support the most ruthless, oppressive regimes so long as they're sufficiently anti-American. Just look at how Obama's new "realism" impressed Norway's Nobel committee, which awarded Obama

the Nobel Peace Prize—right after he characteristically refused
to meet with the Dali Lama in order to avoid offending Communist China.

President Obama needs to learn that the benefits of freedom
are worth the risks—a free Iran could potentially be a close
American ally. Instead, Obama opted to try to make a deal with
the oppressors. Once upon a time, Democrats and Republicans
agreed that America would stand committed to acting on behalf
of democracy and human rights around the world. This bipartisan policy helped to win two world wars and defeat worldwide
Communism, yet these achievements don't seem to impress our
current president. He has decided on a different path.

While Zelaya enjoys the strident support of the Obama
administration, the same cannot be said for some American allies.

In September 2009, President Obama scrapped plans to
install a missile defense shield to protect our Eastern and Central European allies from attack, especially by Iran. Poland and
the Czech Republic had agreed to host the radar and intercep-
tor sites for the missile shield, but Obama decided they could
get by without them. Russia, which had furiously opposed the
missile defense shield from the beginning, applauded Obama's
surrender.

The move was justified by intelligence purporting that Iran's
long-range missile program had not developed as quickly as pro-
jected. It was unfortunate timing, then, that the day news broke
about the missile shield's cancellation, the Associated Press
revealed that a secret report from the world's atomic watchdog,

the International Atomic Energy Agency (IAEA), found Iran "has the ability to make a nuclear bomb and is on the way to developing a missile system able to carry an atomic warhead."

Regardless, the Czech Republic and Poland, two vehemently pro-American countries, were hung out to dry. Having suffered under the boot of Communism for forty years, both nations share a passionate commitment to freedom. They have been close American allies ever since their people rose up and overthrew their Communist overlords twenty years ago. They contributed troops to the U.S. missions in both Iraq and Afghanistan, and they refuse to go along with the America-bashing that dominates some international institutions and even, at times, the European Union.

But that didn't mean much to President Obama. And the Poles and Czechs gleaned a clear message from his actions; as former Czech prime minister Mirek Topolanek said, "The Americans are not interested in this territory as they were before." Or, as the Czech daily *Hospodarske Noviny* put it, "An ally we rely on has betrayed us, and exchanged us for its own, better relations with Russia." In a sure sign of disrespect for Polish sensibilities, President Obama announced the decision to cancel the missile shield on the seventieth anniversary of the Russian invasion of Poland. Perhaps due to the outcry, Obama partly reversed course and announced plans for a scaled-down missile defense shield— one that is far more acceptable to the Russians.

So we have sent a dangerous message to other nations: become an American ally at your own risk, because you might get sold out. Despite the Obama administration's denials, Eastern Europe's defense was clearly sacrificed to appease Russia. Since the shield would have been purely defensive, the Russians didn't have any legitimate complaint: they just wanted to preserve their ability to intimidate their neighbors.

But President Obama has prioritized "resetting" relations with Russia, and our Czech and Polish allies were getting in the way. What's more, President Obama did not even get any concessions from the Russians in return for selling out the Czechs and the Poles. In fact, just after the missile shield's cancellation was announced, the Russian Foreign Ministry clarified that while Russia welcomed the decision, it was not part of any deal between Russia and the United States.

So President Obama surrendered to a key Russian demand and got absolutely nothing in return. To the contrary, the Russians reacted with ill-concealed contempt. Not only have they refused to support stronger sanctions against Iran, but according to Venezuelan madman Hugo Chavez, the Russians have also agreed to help him develop nuclear technology. Former U.S. Ambassador to the UN John Bolton coined a good term for President Obama's handling of this issue: "pre-emptive capitulation."

The disloyalty toward the Czechs and Poles is part of a strange pattern in President Obama's foreign policy. Countries that are the most hostile to America—Iran, Syria, Russia, and Cuba, to name a few—are the objects of a full-on charm offensive. We wine them and dine them, look the other way when they mistreat or kill their own people, give them vital concessions without demanding anything in return, sympathize with their grievances against us, and help end the international isolation many of them rightly experience. Meanwhile, some of our closest allies—the Czechs, the Poles, the Israelis—suddenly find their defense needs are outweighed in Washington by the demands of their enemies.

The long-standing partner in what used to be called our "special relationship," Great Britain, got an early glimpse of this administration's strange foreign policy priorities when British prime minister Gordon Brown, on an early diplomatic visit to newly-elected President Obama, was treated to a curt, scaled-down visit topped off by what seemed a calculated insult. After giving President Obama a gift of a penholder made of wood from an old British naval ship that fought the slave trade, Brown received in return a thoughtless collection of Hollywood DVDs. When asked by Britain's *Sunday Telegraph* about the unenthusiastic welcome for the British prime minister, a State Department official declared, "There's nothing special about Britain. You're just the same as the other 190 countries in the world. You shouldn't expect special treatment."

No, that kind of treatment seems to be reserved for the Iranians and the Russians now.

———————————

Military deterrence is a tried and true concept throughout history—maintain an army so powerful that other countries are afraid to attack it. In other words, keep your army strong so you don't have to use it much. Republicans believe there's a lot of wisdom and common sense in deterrence, but liberals have apparently "moved on."

National security is expensive. But when it comes to defense, Americans would rather spend treasure than blood, especially if all that hardware and know-how intimidates our enemies from attacking us. Still, one of the first things a Democratic president typically does is to slash military spending to help pay for his political wish lists. President Obama is no exception, seeking to finance part of his historic spending spree by hacking $9.4 billion out of the Department of Defense budget. This was part of a much-heralded "scrubbing" in which the administration announced $17 billion in cuts to the federal budget.

President Obama justified the cuts by arguing, "We can no longer afford to spend as if deficits do not matter and waste is not our problem." Apparently deficits did not matter and waste was not our problem when Obama signed the $787 billion stimulus boondoggle. They're only a problem when it comes to national defense.

Of course, if you don't believe America actually has any enemies, then you're not too worried about defense spending. And that's another core problem with today's Democrats: they indulge in a child-like belief that America's enemies are just "friends we haven't met." Liberals think we can sit down across the table from our most implacable foes, show some goodwill, and instantly make them America's buddies. Their unshakable belief in our ability to turn the world's worst miscreants into reliable partners has proven wrong time and time again. They were wrong about Ahmadinejad. They were wrong about Kim Jong-il. They were wrong about Chavez. They were wrong about Fidel and Raul Castro. The world's dictators aren't looking for friends—they openly proclaim that they're looking to weaken the United States and spread revolution.

These dictators portray their violent thuggery as attempts to help "the poor." It's a cruel, sick trick—exploiting genuine suffering to rob entire populations of their freedom, dignity, and basic human rights. But for some reason it gets a good deal of traction

among leftist circles. Michael Moore and other leftwingers proclaim how great things are in Cuba, while overlooking not only the
economic misery that you find in every Communist country, but
the regime's disrespect for human rights. A free press, free elections, free thought, free assembly—such basic rights do not and
cannot exist in thug states. They're characterized by state-run
media, rigged elections, and no protections for freedom of
speech, conscience, or assembly.

These rulers aren't enlightened autocrats who help the down-
trodden. They're gangsters pillaging the freedoms of their coun-
trymen to enrich themselves. They aren't interested in
negotiating honestly with their own people. Why in the world
would they ever negotiate honestly with us?

Liberals, and President Obama in particular, frequently
remind us that many countries in the world have legitimate grievances against past American policies. While few people would
argue that America has never made a mistake, you don't rectify
mistakes by abandoning our nation's commitment to freedom.
Keeping people down won't keep America safe. When Democrats give latitude to oppressors like Chavez and Ahmadinejad as
penance for past American "mistakes," think about who pays the
price. A moment of American humility doesn't do a thing to
relive the suffering of people under the boot of thugs.

It would be nice if we could reason with every one of America's enemies. Successful diplomacy is better than bloodshed, so
negotiation should be our first line of defense whenever possible.

But whether we're talking or fighting, our chance of success increases when we have precise, reliable intelligence.

Though the details can rarely be discussed, well-executed intelligence operations have frequently disrupted bloody terrorist plans here and around the world. That's why Republicans wholeheartedly support a smart, careful, and thorough intelligence program—and why we are so frustrated when Democrats denigrate and misrepresent the work of the intelligence community. When liberals undermine and expose our intelligence efforts, they reduce our alternatives to war.

Here's a notion that until recently was uncontroversial: our government needs to keep secrets. Some secrets help keep our foes in check. Others protect the lives of everyday Americans. But liberals have developed an emotional, instinctive opposition to our own government's preservation of intelligence secrets. And they've decided to do something about it—in 2005 the *New York Times* revealed the Terrorist Surveillance Program, which tracked the international communications of terrorism suspects. The following year, the *Times* and other papers exposed a secret program for monitoring terrorism suspects' banking transactions. And the year after that, the *L.A. Times* detailed a secret CIA effort to get workers on Iran's nuclear program to defect to the United States. As Tony Blankley noted, in some of these cases, there were no allegations at all that the programs were illegal or improper—the papers' editors just felt that the government didn't really have the right to keep secrets.

This bizarre campaign against secrecy continues in Congress today. In summer 2009, House Democrats fulminated

that Congress was "kept out of the loop" by the Bush administration on a never-implemented CIA plan to form paramilitary
groups to kill al Qaeda leaders. Outraged Democrats on the
House Intelligence Committee demanded investigations of Bush
officials—though I didn't hear similar demands to investigate the
Obama administration that September, following a magnificent
commando operation by U.S. special forces in Somalia to assas-
sinate a top al Qaeda terrorist, Saleh Ali Saleh Nabhan.

Of course, the demand to investigate the CIA plan came after
similar demands to investigate nearly every aspect of the Bush
administration's war on terrorism. Democratic stalwart Nancy
Pelosi channeled the moral indignation of her angry leftwing
base and denounced the CIA's terrorist interrogation methods—
methods that yielded valuable intelligence that helped foil active
terrorist plots. When the CIA noted that Pelosi didn't protest
anything when she was briefed about these methods while they
were being used, Pelosi accused the agency of lying.

I'll leave it up to you to decide who's telling the truth here—
the agency that gleaned key intelligence about terrorist plots by
interrogating al Qaeda members, or a leader of the party that is
seeking to prosecute them for doing so.

Liberals may have forgotten the obvious, but I am sure the rest
of America remembers a salient fact: after September 11, we set
out to destroy al Qaeda. I hope we're still at it. As I recall, not long
after September 11, Washington put out a popular deck of fifty-
two playing cards with terrorist leaders on them to show exactly
who we were after. Maybe the liberals had a different deck.

We are talking here about our very lives and the safety of our
families, but for so many on the Left, national security is just

another venue to score partisan points against Republicans. Breezily dismissing the threat of al Qaeda, Iran, and other enemies, these liberals will focus all their attacks on Republicans, because for them Republicans *are* the enemy. They will betray our own secrets, prosecute our own intelligence agents, and endanger our own civilians in order to further their "struggle" against the great enemy at home—the GOP.

There's a reason the American people have for decades considered Democrats weak on defense. It's because they are. When liberals undermine our ability to carry out even the most basic intelligence operations, they reduce our options for peacefully ensuring our security—and make war more likely.

When it comes to national security, here's what separates Republicans from most Democrats: we acknowledge there is evil in the world. It's rare, but it's out there. You can't reason with it, you can't rehabilitate it, and you can't buy it off with groveling apologies. We saw evil in the gas chambers of Nazi Germany; we saw evil in the flames of September 11; we saw evil when Islamic jihadists beheaded journalist Daniel Pearl; and we will see it again.

There are groups and individuals in the world who cannot be reasoned with. They want something, whether it's land or recognition or the supremacy of their religion, and they will do anything to achieve it. They don't play by any rules. They don't recognize human rights, the Geneva Convention, the U.S. Constitution, or any sense of basic morality. And they are overjoyed to hear American leaders insisting that pulling our punches somehow buys us respect in the world. They take it as a sign of American weakness.

By now, they also know that Republicans will fight back smart and hard against America's enemies. We always have and we always will. American security deserves nothing less.

FOUR

WINNING THE VOTE

It's time to fight back. The conservative comeback has already begun, and you ain't seen nothing yet.

STEP

12

Shape Up, Reach Out, and Connect

A Republican Renaissance

WE ARE at a crucial juncture for our party and, more important, for our country.

As the Obama administration spends the country into oblivion, America needs Republican ideas now more than ever. It is time to rise to the occasion and make our voices heard. It is time to serve our country as the loyal opposition.

Denouncing any opposition to President Obama's agenda as unpatriotic or racist, the Democrats want us to be silent. We're even told that opposing the president's policies is, in some crazy way, tantamount to rooting for America's failure.

Of course, you and I know the president's policies are a roadmap to failure. We would be abandoning our responsibility if we were to stand silent while the liberals spend money we don't have, borrow money we will never have, and usher in the most massive expansion of federal government control in the history of the republic.

I've got news for them: we aren't going to be silent. We are going to speak up and show that we have the courage of our convictions. We will support the president when he is doing what is best for America, but we will call him out when he is wrong—and as long as he insists on reckless government spending, we will argue vociferously for a new policy of fiscal responsibility.

It is time for our party to make a fresh start, and it begins now.

WE WILL CHALLENGE THE PRESIDENT OVER THE ISSUES.

We are going to show the nation the harmful results of an administration that is elected on promises of centrism and bipartisanship, then implements an extreme, unworkable liberal agenda. We are going to expose how its policies hurt the country. We are going to give voice to the growing chorus of Americans who understand there is a big difference between creating wealth, and simply taking it from those who earn it and giving it to those who did not. We are not going to be shy about speaking honestly about liberal failure. Simply put, we are going to speak truth to power.

There has been a great deal of talk in Republican circles about how we should deal with this administration and the entire Obama phenomenon. Some Republicans say we need to tiptoe around the president—that we should not take him on, at least not directly. This has led to some handwringing among Republicans and, quite frankly, some missed opportunities. We have seen political professionals urge Republicans to avoid confronting a popular president and to steer clear of any frontal assaults on his administration. Instead, they say we should challenge Speaker of the House Nancy Pelosi...whom nobody likes.

Or Majority Leader Harry Reid...whom nobody knows.

Or Treasury Secretary Tim Geithner...whom nobody believes.

Or the architect of the housing crash, Congressman Barney Frank...whom nobody understands.

They say that in the same way the Democrats target conservative talk show hosts and former vice presidents, we should stick to misdirection. They say that's the only way to fight back, because President Obama is too popular to challenge head-on.

Well, the president *is* personally popular, although that's fading fast. Still, we have to acknowledge his political abilities: he's got an easy demeanor, he's a great orator, his campaign promised vague, happy things like "change" and "hope," he's young, he's cool, he's hip, and he's a great family man. What's not to like? He's got all the qualities America likes in a celebrity, and the press treats him like a superstar.

There's only one problem: he's making some unpopular and unwise decisions that are taking us in the wrong direction and bankrupting our country. Were it not for that little detail, I might be a big fan too.

The president is engaged in the most massive expansion of government our country has ever seen. He is spending America into debt of such mammoth proportions that none of us can even begin to calculate it or really understand it. A trillion dollars here, a trillion dollars there—the numbers seem unreal.

We will and we must stand against these disastrous policies, regardless of the president's popularity. The candidate who campaigned in favor of a bottom-up style of governing is presiding over an enormous, top-down expansion of government bureaucracy and spending. American government is not a game, not a popularity contest, and not a political version of *American Idol*.

Candidate Obama promised to work for compromise with Republicans, but President Obama is governing so far to the left he's making the Carter administration look like a bastion of conservatism.

Candidate Obama talked about fiscal responsibility and forcing government to live within its means, but President Obama is saddling our children and grandchildren with mountains of debt.

Candidate Obama promised to cut taxes (at least for some), but President Obama is trying to ram through the largest tax increases in history to pay for his massive expansion of government. Some of these taxes may be disguised, such as his cap-and-trade scheme, but we Republicans know a job-killing tax when we see one.

Candidate Obama promised bipartisanship, but President Obama could not be more partisan. He is carrying water for radical fringe groups such as ACORN and for anti-growth environmental extremists.

So what is the loyal opposition to do?

We are going to confront Democratic power and hegemony with Republican principles, policies, and ideas. The honeymoon for the liberals and for President Obama is over. We are going to challenge policies that are wrong—without apology and without hesitation. We have a simple goal: success for America.

And within our own party, we need to make it clear that from now on there will be a price to pay for abandoning conservative principles. The grassroots—activists from tea parties to town-halls—have sent a message: no more "fake-it-until-you-make-it" conservatives. The days of merely espousing conservative principles and then, once elected, governing or legislating without principle, are over. At least one senator has already got this message—Arlen Specter. In early 2009, after years of distressing votes for big government, Specter's vote for the stimulus bill provoked an outcry among Pennsylvania's Republican grassroots. Having barely survived a 2004 primary challenge from principled conservative Pat Toomey, Specter asked me what he could do to mend fences with conservatives. I said he needed to stand with us against card check (which abolishes the secret ballot on forming unions) and against the cap-and-trade carbon cutting scheme. He agreed, publicly declaring himself against those proposals—and soon after, he abandoned the party and became a Democrat.

All the talk about pushing Specter out of the party, or making it hard for him to stay, was just bunk. For him, the politics of reelection outweighed taking any principled position on the issues. Since then he has switched his position on card check, and I won't be surprised if he switches on cap-and-trade. He exposed himself as a political opportunist, and we don't need political opportunists in our party. If he survives his next primary, my goal will be to retire him.

One more thing. In contrast to the Democrats' ugly and personal attacks over the last eight years, Republicans are going to challenge this president with class, respecting both his dignity and our own. He is not our enemy, he is our political opponent—and he is still our president. I know this is a foreign concept to most liberals, and it is a sharp contrast to the shabby, vulgar way they attacked President Bush. But we will focus our critique squarely on the president's policies. We will simply explain why his policies are misguided and propose better ones. With such a stunning array of wrong-headed policies to choose from, we have no need to resort to personal cheap-shots.

The mainstream media fawns over President Obama, even as they swear up and down that they're objective. But occasionally one of them will say what's really on their mind. In summer 2009, *Newsweek* editor Evan Thomas told MSNBC that "in a way, Obama's standing above the country, above—above the world. He's sort of God."

No word yet on where Evan wants to build the first Church of Obama.

Shortly after President Obama's election, MSNBC's Chris Matthews had this exchange with Joe Scarborough:

> **Matthews:** I want to do everything I can to make this thing work, this new presidency work, and I think that—

> **Scarborough:** Is that your job? You just talked
> about being a journalist!
> **Matthews:** Yeah, it is my job.

We really ought to thank Matthews. Instead of denying his fervor for Obama like most journalists do, Chris owns up to his spin. Maybe he could be the pastor at Evan's new church.

When ABC set aside an hour of its primetime programming for a "special" that was really an infomercial for Democratic plans for socialized medicine, Rush Limbaugh nailed it. He stopped referring to the "drive-by media" and started calling them the "state-run media." Sounds about right to me.

Still, I wouldn't break ground on the Capitol mall for an Obama monument just yet, for there is increasing opposition to his policies among the American people. Most working Americans and their families don't give two hoots about popularity polls, Chris Matthews' crushes, or who the gang at *Newsweek* prays to. The American people are concerned about jobs, foreclosures, bailouts, taxes, spending, debt, and national security.

The last Democratic president, Bill Clinton, declared that the era of big government was over. Can someone please send President Obama a copy of that speech? Because the new Democratic president has ushered in an era of unprecedented leftwing, old-school, top-down, industrial-age, bureaucratic, ever-expanding government.

Ignore the Obama administration's happy talk about jobs "saved" or some other unmeasureable and unknowable nonsense. In the first six months after Obama took office with a Democratic majority in the House and Senate, nearly three million people were thrown out of work. The extravagant "stimulus" hasn't done a thing for Americans except put our children's children deeper into debt. Meanwhile, millions of Americans are wondering why all that spending and taxing and borrowing didn't save their jobs.

Americans should ask the president and the liberal Congress why they could find hundreds of billions of dollars for make-work projects, to buy shares of banks run by their fat-cat friends, and to take over the car industry while the unemployment rate shot past 10 percent. So much for all these spending programs that we were told we just *had* to pass in order to create jobs.

Liberals are ushering in a new America where more people are moving down the ladder of opportunity than are moving up. They are bringing about an America that is less industrious and less ambitious than it was in previous generations. They are creating a new culture of dependency.

This is the worst of liberal fringe-thinking. Its advocates have seized control of the Democratic Party. And now that party is running the nation.

THE REPUBLICAN COMEBACK HAS BEGUN, AND IT STARTS IN THE HEARTLAND, NOT WASHINGTON, D.C.

The last few years have not been easy for our party, but the Republican comeback is underway. In every part of the country, Republican leaders and conservative, grassroots Americans are gaining in strength and number. They are speaking candidly about what the nation needs and what our party should be doing.

They are reviewing our strategies and tactics, learning from each other, and speaking their minds about how best to reach common goals. From Oregon to Idaho, from Wisconsin to Indiana, from Florida to Georgia, the energy at the grassroots is strong—and growing stronger.

The chattering classes inside the Beltway are too busy fretting over phony disputes and intra-party intrigue—and fighting over the spoils of all this taxing and borrowing—to notice that a change has indeed come to America. But it's not the one President Obama had in mind.

If you live outside Washington, D.C., you know what I'm talking about. Those of you who attend Lincoln Day dinners and county party events—you know. Those of you who "toil in the vineyards," so to speak, spending time in communities, in diners, barber shops, and coffee shops—you know. Those of you who spend time not with political consultants and yes-men but with people who work for a living—you know. Those of you who want to be able to count on government when it's supposed to help and want it to stay out of the way the rest of the time—you know. The change is underway. You can see it and feel it. And you know it.

Early in 2009, that change came at "tea parties" held from coast to coast to protest this administration's out-of-control spending. That was only the first wave. By summer, that change came from townhall meetings at which average Janes and Joes expressed their outrage at the prospect of government-run healthcare. In September, tens of thousands of taxpayers—perhaps hundreds of thousands of them—from across the nation descended on Washington, D.C., for a huge protest against irresponsible spending and expanding government control. And in November, the voters threw the Democrats out of the governors' mansions in Virginia and New Jersey, putting principled conservatives in their place.

Our comeback is not beginning in Washington, and our conversation with America is not focused on Washington. Our party is looking beyond Washington—to the American people.

HERE'S WHERE THE REPUBLICAN PARTY IS HEADED.

The Republican Party is grounded in the ideas and character of Edmund Burke, William F. Buckley, and Ronald Reagan. I trace my own conservative roots to these men. Each of them demanded that conservatism always respect reality, effectively assess the times, and stay relevant to the era. Thus is our charge today.

Ronald Reagan insisted that our party always move aggressively to seize the moment. He challenged us to recognize the truth of the times and live by first principles in both word and deed. As conservatives, we must stop acting like we don't really believe in our principles. If we are right, what do we have to fear?

In this hour, conservatives stand a bit stronger, a bit wiser— ready once again to think and act with conviction and boldness. For conservatism to take root in the next generation we must offer wise, fair, and practical solutions to the nation's current problems.

A Republican renaissance has begun.

America conquered the challenges of the last century, emerging as the world's only superpower. Now it is time to conquer the challenges of today. Our success will not be found in dusting off campaign manuals from years past. Instead, we will achieve success by speaking directly to the American people about a rebirth of the American dream for this generation and generations to come.

Our voice has been and must once again be a reflection of the character and wisdom of the majority of Americans. It is up to us to expose the great Democratic fraud that is now being thrust upon this nation. Personal freedom, liberty, and free enterprise are the timeless values that Americans hold dear—and President Obama and the liberals are brazenly pushing them aside.

In our Declaration of Independence, Thomas Jefferson wrote that we are endowed by God with certain unalienable rights, including life, liberty, and the pursuit of happiness. Those rights are not conferred upon us by the federal government, but by a greater power. Yet the Democrats act as if the government is the source of liberty, with the arbitrary power to constrict our freedom at will. They could not be more wrong.

Republicans—and most Americans—know that no politician or president, no matter how popular, can give those rights to us. They are ours by birth. It is time to stand up against those who are infringing upon them—and make no mistake, that is exactly what they are doing.

As Republicans, we will stand up for everyday Americans who worry about their bills, who find themselves defenseless against economic hardship, who want to know what in the world has happened to an American government that used to trust the people and help preserve a level playing field. Now is the time to organize ourselves and to demand the limited government and freedom that is every American's birthright.

As Republicans we will act decisively. We will offer real solutions, and we will do so aggressively and without apology. We will champion individual freedom and individual responsibility.

I am used to working against the odds imposed on us by critics, pundits, and other clueless elites. I am confident in this journey because I am taking it with like-minded people around the nation. I gain strength in this journey from people who care about America in the same way I do. A Republican renaissance has begun, our opportunities lie before us, and our cause is as true and just today as when we first began in 1854.

In the best spirit of President Reagan, it's time to saddle up and ride. Our country needs us.

APPENDIX

1

Excerpted here is a speech I gave to the Ronald Reagan Conservative Society on February 2, 2008.

WHAT A GREAT honor to be here with you all this evening.

I have great optimism for the future of the conservative movement and our nation.

But that optimism is tempered by the realities of war and the signs of the challenges that lie ahead for us at home and abroad.

The vitriolic rhetoric and heavy-handed tactics so far this campaign season have become a symbol for all that turns voters off.

So, I'd like to set the tone for this afternoon with a quote from Frederick Douglass.

Mr. Douglass once noted, "I glory in conflict that I may hereafter exult in victory." I like that!

As a black, Roman Catholic, conservative Republican from Maryland, I know a little bit about conflict.

But today, what conflicts us is not ups and downs of elections, but rather the very nature of conservatism in this post-Reagan era. What conflicts us is the vision of the conservative movement, its radical nature, and the unique challenges and opportunities that come from both conflict and victory.

Our world has changed. America has changed.

And the leaders of America must demonstrate they are prepared to lead in these changing times with vision, strength, and humility.

We quickly realize there is no magic formula, no secret potion or handshake that will make you or the conservative movement more attractive, let alone acceptable, to minority or majority communities in North Carolina or anywhere else.

The greatest opportunity for success lies not in convincing people we don't bite, but rather in our ability to demonstrate our genuine concerns for the scourge of drugs and crime gripping our states; for the reach of a government that increasingly inserts itself into our lives; for the family struggling to live paycheck to paycheck; for the continual erosion of our constitutional rights; for the corruption of our school systems; and for the weakening of our families and the taking of human life—born and unborn.

In the twenty-first century, we have the opportunity to say and do something radical about what we believe.

But today we stand on the precipice of conservatism, ready to throw each other off because of those beliefs. We feel as if we've lost our grip on what conservatism means; indeed, what it means to be a Republican.

But the core of who we are and what we believe has not changed. Conservatives believe first and foremost in the power and ingenuity of the individual to create the legacy of a nation through hard work and self-discipline.

Conservatives believe that government should be limited so that it never becomes powerful enough to infringe on the rights of the individual.

Conservatives believe in low taxes so that individuals might keep more of their own money, and the economic power that it represents.

Conservatives believe in business regulations that encourage entrepreneurs to take risks so that more individuals can enjoy the satisfaction and fruits of self-made success.

Conservatives believe in the ideal of a colorblind society, so that each man or woman is treated as an individual and not as a member of some hyphenated class or group.

Remember, my friends, Democrats just talk about change; we consciously act to bring about the change this nation needs.

As people dedicated to the fight for freedom and equality, Republicans have always been on the frontlines of making change real for all Americans.

But as this new century unfolds it is important that we have in place a new generation of leaders who understand the difference between giving a person a fish and teaching that person how to fish; between just giving hope and turning their hopes into action.

For years, I sat in audiences and listened as liberals tried to win over voters, especially minority voters, by talking about hope.

"Hope is on the way," "Keep hope alive," "Hope you have a nice day!" Sound familiar?

The illiterate, the suffering, the addicted, the homeless—they demand more from leaders than "hope" because hope by itself is neither a strategy nor a solution.

Hope by itself won't protect you from terrorists, or lower your taxes, or pay your bills. Hope by itself will not buy you a home nor ensure quality education for your kids.

Without action, hope passively waits on others to solve problems.

Without action, hope looks to next year instead of doing the hard work required today. Without action, hope is powerless to transform lives.

So we must act, and as this election unfolds, conservatives must act in a genuine way to demonstrate the truth of America: that every American regardless of his or her station in life, upbringing, or social status has the opportunity to turn their hopes into action and to realize the promise that is the American dream.

We live in an exciting time, my friends, and our mission has not changed since 1854. It remains to empower the people of this great nation to no longer hope in vain, but to put their hopes into action.

So as the party of Lincoln stood with those whose hands and feet were shackled over a century ago, today we must stand with those who are shackled by the soft bigotry of low expectations in education, the dehumanizing effects of addiction, and the hopelessness of lost opportunity at the hands of an opportunistic government.

Ronald Reagan understood that, and he acted to lift a dispirited nation to become that "shining city on a hill."

As a young man, I was always struck by Ronald Reagan's unwavering optimism for America. For me, that sense of "our best days lie before us" was captured in the phrase, "Morning in America." Although that was in 1984, for Democrats in 2008 it's more like lunchtime in America.

But you and I know what Ronald Reagan knew: that the promise of America is the promise of endless possibilities, and that promise values the freedom of the human spirit to access fully the opportunities of America.

I know that many of you share in this passion, this radical vision of our conservative cause.

So, let's work to define this vision in a radical agenda for the twenty-first century; an agenda that seeks to empower not by creating dependency, but by creating opportunities for future generations.

Let's define for America those values we hold dear: the value to the soul of religious faith, complete integrity, loyalty, and truthfulness. Let's honor America with incorruptible public service, a respect for economy in government, self-reliance, thrift, and individual liberty. Let's stand firm in our patriotism, real love of country, and willingness to sacrifice for it as those who have gone before us.

Let's start acting like Republicans again!

Remember: our challenge will lie not in beating liberals (although that can be fun too), but in not beating ourselves. We forgot that and paid a dear price for it in 2006.

Oh, by the way, if you see Hillary Clinton, please tell her there is no "rightwing conspiracy," only the right way to uplift a people and transform a nation, and it's not by raising their taxes, redistributing their wealth, or giving illegal immigrants a driver's license. That goes for you too, Barack!

So, my friends, it is not yet lunchtime in America. It is morning again. And in a sense, it will always be morning in America, because America *is* morning. It is a place of eternal promise and potential.

It is this quality more than any other that makes America special. America will always be the one place on earth where possibility meets opportunity. We call that the American dream.

For countless Americans, my friends, this dream inspires us to embrace the values that shape us, transform us, and make us free.

The old rules no longer apply, my friends, and when that happens, we will glory in conflict that we may truly exult in victory!

God bless each of you. And may God continue to bless and guide our president, the men and women serving in harms way for our sake, and may God bless in a special way this grand experiment we call America!

APPENDIX

2

Some Republicans today say we need to move on from Ronald Reagan. I'm not one of them. Below is a rendition of Reagan's 1964 "A Time for Choosing" speech in support of Barry Goldwater's presidential campaign. The themes of the speech—overbearing government, attempts to socialize medicine, mendacious efforts by liberals to present big government policies as a form of humanitarianism—ring true to conservatives in the age of Obama.

A Time for Choosing

I AM GOING to talk of controversial things. I make no apology for this.

It's time we asked ourselves if we still know the freedoms intended for us by the Founding Fathers. James Madison said, "We base all our experiments on the capacity of mankind for self government."

This idea—that government was beholden to the people, that it had no other source of power—is still the newest, most unique

idea in all the long history of man's relation to man. This is the
issue of this election: Whether we believe in our capacity for self-
government or whether we abandon the American Revolution
and confess that a little intellectual elite in a far-distant capital
can plan our lives for us better than we can plan them ourselves.

You and I are told we must choose between a left or right, but
I suggest there is no such thing as a left or right. There is only an
up or down. Up to man's age-old dream—the maximum of individual freedom consistent with order—or down to the ant heap
of totalitarianism. Regardless of their sincerity, their humanitar-
ian motives, those who would sacrifice freedom for security have
embarked on this downward path. Plutarch warned, "The real
destroyer of the liberties of the people is he who spreads among
them bounties, donations and benefits."

The Founding Fathers knew a government can't control the
economy without controlling people. And they knew when a government sets out to do that, it must use force and coercion to
achieve its purpose. So we have come to a time for choosing.

Public servants say, always with the best of intentions, "What
greater service we could render if only we had a little more
money and a little more power." But the truth is that outside of
its legitimate function, government does nothing as well or as
economically as the private sector.

Yet any time you and I question the schemes of the do-
gooders, we're denounced as being opposed to their humanitar-
ian goals. It seems impossible to legitimately debate their solutions
with the assumption that all of us share the desire to help the less
fortunate. They tell us we're always "against," never "for" anything.

We are for a provision that destitution should not follow unemployment by reason of old age, and to that end we have accepted Social Security as a step toward meeting the problem. However, we are against those entrusted with this program when they practice deception regarding its fiscal shortcomings, when they charge that any criticism of the program means that we want to end payments. . . .

We are for aiding our allies by sharing our material blessings with nations which share our fundamental beliefs, but we are against doling out money government to government, creating bureaucracy, if not socialism, all over the world.

We need true tax reform that will at least make a start toward restoring for our children the American Dream that wealth is denied to no one, that each individual has the right to fly as high as his strength and ability will take him. . . . But we cannot have such reform while our tax policy is engineered by people who view the tax as a means of achieving changes in our social structure. . . .

Have we the courage and the will to face up to the immorality and discrimination of the progressive tax, and demand a return to traditional proportionate taxation? . . . Today in our country the tax collector's share is 37 cents of every dollar earned. Freedom has never been so fragile, so close to slipping from our grasp.

Are you willing to spend time studying the issues, making yourself aware, and then conveying that information to family and friends? Will you resist the temptation to get a government handout for your community? Realize that the doctor's fight against socialized medicine is your fight. We can't socialize the doctors without socializing the patients. Recognize that government invasion of public power is eventually an assault upon your own business. If some among you fear taking a stand because you are afraid of reprisals from customers, clients, or even government, recognize that you are just feeding the crocodile hoping he'll eat you last.

If all of this seems like a great deal of trouble, think what's at stake. We are faced with the most evil enemy mankind has known in his long climb from the swamp to the stars. There can be no security anywhere in the free world if there is no fiscal and economic stability within the United States. Those who ask us to trade our freedom for the soup kitchen of the welfare state are architects of a policy of accommodation.

They say the world has become too complex for simple answers. They are wrong. There are no easy answers, but there are simple answers. We must have the courage to do what we know is morally right. Winston Churchill said that "the destiny of man is not measured by material computation. When great forces are on the move in the world, we learn we are spirits—not animals." And he said, "There is something going on in time and space, and beyond time and space, which, whether we like it or not, spells duty."

You and I have a rendezvous with destiny. We will preserve for our children this, the last best hope of man on earth, or we will sentence them to take the first step into a thousand years of darkness. If we fail, at least let our children and our children's children say of us we justified our brief moment here. We did all that could be done.

INDEX